"As a woman who has fought anxiety most c
you're in a battle, it's not a reason for guilt o
a warrior. I've also learned having the right w
Anxiety's Grip will encourage and equip yo
more victory."

Holley Gerth, bestselling author of *What Your Heart Needs*
for the Hard Days

"My listeners love to hear from Dr. Bengtson because she expresses empathy
and understanding and provides practical and specific solutions to the daily
anxieties that can plague us. This book not only turns our focus back to the
Bible but applies its timeless wisdom to our lives in a very real and pragmatic
way; it is truly a road map toward peace."

Jeff Angelo, talk show host, Newsradio 1040 WHO, iHeartMedia

"Life is hard. At times, worry and fear seem the only logical response. But
there is a peace that passes understanding available if we'll just reach out
and take it. In *Breaking Anxiety's Grip*, Dr. Michelle Bengtson offers expert
advice that's both practical and biblical, helping us navigate life's difficulties
as we tap into the promises of God."

Joanna Weaver, author of *Having a Mary Heart in a Martha World:*
Finding Intimacy with God in the Busyness of Life

"If you've ever been strangled by anxiety, if you've awakened at night in
a panic, if worry has become your constant, frustrating companion, then
find the hope, instruction, and wisdom you need in the pages of *Breaking
Anxiety's Grip* by Dr. Michelle Bengtson. As a therapist, she brings astute
counsel. As someone who has endured many stressors, she brings the wisdom
that comes from endurance. And as a fellow struggler, she brings empathy.
In these pages, you will find help and hope."

Mary DeMuth, author of *Healing Every Day: A 90-Day*
Devotional Journey

"If you are looking to eradicate the power that anxiety has over your life,
you might consider a good counselor. Or you might look for someone who's
been through what you're facing now. Perhaps you'd seek out a trusted friend.
What if I told you that you could have all three? That's what you get in
Breaking Anxiety's Grip. Dr. Michelle Bengtson is all of that—and more."

Jennifer Dukes Lee, author of *It's All Under Control*
and *The Happiness Dare*

"Reading Dr. Michelle Bengtson's book *Breaking Anxiety's Grip* is like talking to a trusted friend. Her voice throughout the book will calm and reassure
you in life's daily difficult challenges. Worry, anxiety, and fear are plaguing

America, and Michelle deals with the topic head-on while giving both a clinical and biblical perspective for the 'common cold' of mental health."

Marta Greenman, Words of Grace & Truth, GraceAndTruthRadio.World

"Nowhere else have I found an author to speak to the common struggles with worry, anxiety, and fear with as much professional authority, personal insight, care, and compassion. Reading *Breaking Anxiety's Grip* is like having both a trusted friend and a personal counselor take you by the hand while you rely on God's Word and his faithful promises to victoriously overcome!"

Amy Elaine Martinez, host of *Real Victory Radio*, author of *Becoming a Victory Girl*, and writer at amyelaine.com

"Every once in a while we come across a book that looks at everyday issues from a new and enlightened vantage point and helps remove the blinders that have kept us enslaved to problems. *Breaking Anxiety's Grip* is one of those books. We have all suffered from the effects of worry, anxiety, and fear at some point. Dr. Bengtson takes a unique but biblically based perspective on how to rid ourselves of their slavery in our lives and live from a position of peace. This will be a book to share with family, friends, church leaders, and counselors so that together we can break the hold anxiety has in our lives."

Michelle Wilson, senior producer of *The 700 Club*

"We live in a culture of strife and disagreement. Yet everyone can agree that life is stressful and anxiety is our constant companion. Dr. Michelle Bengtson tackles these issues head-on and gives readers the tools to do the same thing. The pages of this book are filled with gentle insight and tough love that point us to the One who gives the peace we all crave. This will be a book that will become dog-eared with love and one I'll pass on again and again."

Edie Melson, director of the Blue Ridge Mountains Christian Writers Conference

"In *Breaking Anxiety's Grip*, the truth of God's Word coupled with the perspective of a medical professional sheds light on a peace that is possible. This how-to book is conversational and relational, backed by clinical facts and biblical truth. The peace of God transcends our understanding, but that doesn't mean it isn't possible. Breaking anxiety's grip really is a process that requires some action on our part. Michelle gives us the steps to take to reclaim that peace and gently takes our hand and walks through it with us."

Eryn Hall, director of Declare and author at mamahall.com

"*Breaking Anxiety's Grip* is a great encouragement and tool for those who reside in the 'what ifs.' Dr. Michelle Bengtson shows her readers how to move from worry, anxiety, and fear to hope, trust, and peace. This book offers biblically sound and effective practices to loosen anxiety's grip in order to find peace in the palm of God's hand."

Lori Wildenberg, speaker and author of five books, including *The Messy Life of Parenting*

"In *Breaking Anxiety's Grip*, Dr. Bengtson enhances the current work on the topics of worry, anxiety, and fear by adding an intentionally spiritual approach while not ignoring the contributing physical and psychosocial factors. I love the reflective application questions given at the end of each chapter and am excited to add this title to our counseling center's list of faith-based recommendations."

Michelle Nietert, MA, LPC-S; clinical director of Community Counseling Associates, *Living Magazine*'s Best Therapy Center

"Dr. B has done it again. Laced with personal experiences that illustrate the truth of God's Word over the enemy's lies, which stir up worry, anxiety, fear, and doubt, this message is timely and profound. What you hold in your hands is a proven strategy to be victorious over the schemes of Satan in your life. A death blow to the kingdom of darkness, *Breaking Anxiety's Grip* is a resource designed to set the captives free from the bondage of fear in all its facets. Buy a dozen copies, one for yourself and eleven to give away to those you love the most. You won't regret it!"

Athena Dean Holtz, publisher at Redemption Press, author advocate, publishing pioneer

"In an age where anxiety abounds, Dr. Michelle Bengtson gently takes the hands of readers on a step-by-step journey to find freedom from fear through the power of God's perfect love. Her authenticity is refreshing. Her insight is empowering. My own 'aha!' moments came one after another. In a word— WOW! For anyone ready to cultivate the courage to become all God created you to be and live in his peace, this is your book."

Aliene Thompson, Treasured Ministries

"*Breaking Anxiety's Grip* shows how to scripturally break the strongholds of worry and fear in a world filled with doubt and distrust in God's provision. Learn how to battle the enemy with eternal truths and exchange the worldview that embraces lies and momentary pleasures with a deeper faith and God's peace."

DiAnn Mills, author of *Fatal Strike*, www.diannmills.com

"Worry, anxiety, and fear take a huge toll on our bodies and relationships. Dr. Bengtson has written an excellent book on how to overcome these significant stressors, and she gives you a pathway to reclaim a peace-filled life.

You will want to read this book! This will be a helpful resource for readers, teachers, counselors, and ministry leaders."

Nancy Houston, LPC, author of *Love and Sex: A Christian Guide to Human Sexuality*

"As a diagnosed bipolar for twenty years, my one earnest prayer has been, 'God, please send more workers to the mental-health field!' (Matt. 9:37). That prayer is being answered through people like Dr. Michelle Bengtson, a board certified neuropsychologist with thirty years of professional experience in mental health who also understands from her own personal struggles and revelation. To pastors, spouses, teachers, parents, principals, psychologists, and psychiatrists: this book is a resource for your leadership AND a gift for anyone under your care struggling and searching for a breakthrough. God bless you, Michelle, for writing this! Thank you, Lord, for hearing my prayers!"

Heather Palacios, Church by the Glades, WondHerful.com

"My friend Dr. Michelle Bengtson has written another book that has the precision of a laser when addressing worry, anxiety, and fear. As she did with *Hope Prevails*, Michelle takes a topic that many of us struggle with and demystifies the stigma surrounding it. I believe having both *Hope Prevails* and *Breaking Anxiety's Grip* in your library will enable you to understand and combat two of the most prevalent mental health issues facing humanity today."

Tim Ross, lead pastor of Embassy City Church, Dallas, TX

"Can you imagine what life would be like without any worry, anxiety, or fear? In *Breaking Anxiety's Grip*, Dr. Bengtson shares from her professional expertise and personal experience how we can have a life governed by the peace God promises rather than unsettling and often paralyzing worry and anxiety. I speak to and hear from women weekly who have almost given up ever having an anxiety-free life. I am so thankful to have *Breaking Anxiety's Grip* to put in their hands as a tool."

Christi Miranda, founder of Preach Girl! and My Collective

"Life is filled with changes that keep many in a constant state of anxiety. In *Breaking Anxiety's Grip*, Dr. Michelle Bengtson speaks intimately about her personal experience with fear and practically on how to replace it with the truth of God's Word. Through an engaging use of Scripture and powerful use of storytelling, Michelle invites us to exchange our persistent worries with lasting peace. If you struggle with trusting God in the middle of challenging times, this book is for you."

Saundra Dalton-Smith, MD, author of *Sacred Rest*

Breaking
Anxiety's
Grip

Also by Michelle Bengtson

*Hope Prevails: Insights from a Doctor's Personal
Journey through Depression*

Hope Prevails Bible Study

Breaking Anxiety's Grip

*How to Reclaim the Peace
God Promises*

DR. MICHELLE
BENGTSON

Revell

a division of Baker Publishing Group
Grand Rapids, Michigan

© 2019 by Dr. Michelle Bengtson

Published by Revell
a division of Baker Publishing Group
PO Box 6287, Grand Rapids, MI 49516-6287
www.revellbooks.com

Printed in the United States of America

Library of Congress Cataloging-in-Publication Data

Names: Bengtson, Michelle, author.
Title: Breaking anxiety's grip : how to reclaim the peace God promises / Dr. Michelle Bengtson.
Description: Grand Rapids : Revell, a division of Baker Publishing Group, 2019. | Includes bibliographical references.
Identifiers: LCCN 2019002506 | ISBN 9780800735937 (pbk.)
Subjects: LCSH: Anxiety—Religious aspects—Christianity. | Peace—Religious aspects—Christianity.
Classification: LCC BV4908.5 .B46 2019 | DDC 248.8/6—dc23
LC record available at https://lccn.loc.gov/2019002506

19 20 21 22 23 24 25   7 6 5 4 3 2 1

To my husband, Scott. You have given me wind beneath my wings to embrace the purposes, plans, and call God has had on my life. I love you, and I thank you for who you are and all you've done to always support my every dream and goal with your blessing to "go, do, and be all that God has called you to." You have repeatedly demonstrated through your words and actions how to relinquish worry, anxiety, and fear in order to fully embrace God's gift of peace. Our life together has been a testimony of God's goodness and faithfulness. May it always be.

Contents

The Longing for Peace

Deadlines looming, job demands and instability, financial insufficiency, children's poor decisions, relationship discord, military deployment, the stress of social media distraction and comparisons, the fear of missing out, and more things to do than hours in a day. Sound familiar? This is the breeding ground for worry, anxiety, and fear.

In *Breaking Anxiety's Grip*, I've written the words I needed to hear, words I needed to heed throughout my life, and still do. I pray these words will also resonate with the one who is sinking in the midst of the storm, the one whose stomach churns, the one who suffers restless, sleepless nights, and the one whose mind is not at rest and not at peace.

We lack but long for peace. We struggle to live at peace with ourselves, our circumstances, and others. We wrestle with insecurity, inadequacy, comparison, control, worry, anxiety, and fear.

As I sit in my private practice office, so much confusion, sadness, worry, and despair walks in with each patient every day—from the mother whose child keeps getting in trouble at school to the couple who is considering divorce to the adult child or spouse who is watching as their loved one's memories dwindle due to dementia.

I see it in their eyes. They are weary and searching, worried, anxious, and overwhelmed. They crave normalcy and stability. They long for answers, direction, and comfort. They crave peace. Maybe you do too.

"Just tell me it will be okay."

"Comfort me and confirm that we will survive this."

"Tell us what to do and where to go for the help we don't even know we need."

"Help us find peace."

My goal for you is that you will experience peace from the God of hope. The apostle Paul describes it this way: "May the God of hope fill you with all joy and peace as you trust in him, so that you may overflow with hope by the power of the Holy Spirit" (Rom. 15:13). My desire is that you, or someone you care about, will come face-to-face with the God of hope and with his Son, the Prince of Peace.

I had just sent off my manuscript of *Hope Prevails: Insights from a Doctor's Personal Journey through Depression* and had asked God what I should write about next. I hoped the answer would be something much lighter than the subject I had just finished writing about: depression. I was thinking along the lines of the prettiest beaches or most interesting lighthouses in Michigan, or something delicious and lighthearted like chocolate or iced tea. I find peace in chocolate and at the beach . . . but it's not lasting peace.

When I sensed the familiar still, small voice prompting me with my next book idea—exchanging worry, anxiety, and fear for his peace—my initial reaction was "Lord, are you sure?"

As I sensed him prompting me to pen *Breaking Anxiety's Grip*, I winced, as I realized the first thing that needed to happen was for me to shed my anxiety over writing a book about anxiety.

I know how fear takes hold and paralyzes even the ready and willing writer. I feared:

This book wouldn't be as good as my previous book.

It wouldn't meet readers' needs.

It would be my thoughts and words, not God's . . . the only ones that matter.

Maybe I wouldn't really know what I was talking about.

It wouldn't meet the publisher's expectations.

The editor's proverbial red pen wouldn't be kind.

I had to surrender my fears and trust that this was God's project and that he would see it through to completion with words that would help, heal, and free the reader from worry, anxiety, and fear.

Breaking Anxiety's Grip was written for you, from my professional expertise but also from my personal experience of following God's leading as I sought to exchange my worry, anxiety, and fear for his peace. But first I wrote for an audience of one. I wrote for God. In obedience to his call. His words were the words I sought. His words offer healing. His words bring comfort and rest and freedom. His words give peace.

I long to look worry, anxiety, and fear in the eye and laugh. I desire contentment with where God has me, without needing to know his plan. When difficult situations come, I desire to turn my back on worry, anxiety, and fear and retain my peace, trusting that God has allowed the difficulties for my good rather than feeling betrayed and abandoned by him in the storm. I desire these things for you as well.

My prayer for you is this:

> *I long to look worry, anxiety, and fear in the eye and laugh. I desire contentment with where God has me, without needing to know his plan.*

Lord, you are not the author of confusion, sadness, or despair. You came so that we might have abundant life. You came to give us peace despite our situations and circumstances. I pray that as readers take in this book, they might learn to leave their worries, anxieties, and fears with you and take a bit of your peace with them. In Jesus's name, amen.

Music has encouraged me through some very dark and frightening times and has been an inspiration to my mind, heart, and spirit. Because of that, at the end of each chapter, I have included a recommended playlist of songs to encourage you. To get you started, you might enjoy listening to the following:

"My Prayer for You," Alisa Turner, © 2017 by Integrity Music

"You're Gonna Be OK," Jenn Johnson and Brian Johnson, ℗© 2017 by Bethel Music

At the end of each chapter, I have also included a doctor's prescription ("Your Rx") with questions to help you personalize and apply the material from the chapter to your own situation.

Worry, anxiety, and fear impact us physically, emotionally, and spiritually. This book primarily focuses on the spiritual side of worry, anxiety, and fear, a component often left out of most books. As a neuropsychologist who has treated patients with depression and anxiety for nearly three decades, I must underscore that there are also physical and emotional components. Please do not hesitate to consult with a physician or psychiatrist for medication or with a psychologist or counselor for therapy if the need exists.

I pray this book encourages you, emboldens you, and guides you toward a life of peace you might not have even thought possible. I pray that as you read this message, you will become aware of your experience of worry, anxiety, and fear and that you, too, will choose to let it all go into the hands of our precious Savior and be set free. Worry, anxiety, and fear are not your portion, but peace is!

Peace Prevails,
Dr. Michelle

1

The Elephant in the Room

Search me, God, and know my heart;
test me and know my anxious thoughts.

Psalm 139:23

Every tomorrow has two handles. We can take hold of it with
the handle of anxiety or the handle of faith.

Henry Ward Beecher

His lips quivered, and his eyes filled with mist that threatened to
overflow like Niagara Falls. Physically, he was on the verge of man-
hood but suddenly, he looked like the young boy he really was: meek,
timid, and afraid. My youngest son was reaching toward adulthood
while still clinging to childhood, but either way he was too young for
the fearful thoughts now running through his mind.

Next to him sat my oldest son, trying hard to maintain eye contact
but afraid to sustain it for fear that the tears would come and then
his younger brother would be assured there was reason for his fears.
His voice was but a whisper as he acknowledged our words. Shifting
mechanically, almost robotically, unable to get comfortable, almost

out of reverence for the gravity of what he had just been told, he held himself up on the bed on one stiff arm.

Never imagining having to tell my children such difficult words, I felt prickly tears flow down my cheeks, past my chin, and down my knotted neck. Unable to offer any promises or certainty, no cotton candy or pony rides, no sunshine or rainbows, I could only give warm hugs. Yet all the while my mind raced with anxiety-induced strategic plans faster than a Pentagon planning session: alerting loved ones, planning freezer meals, rearranging my office schedule, canceling conferences and travel—in short, attempting to cope with the changes and interruptions soon to come.

How would my family and I handle this gut-wrenching ordeal we were facing? Cancer doesn't affect just those diagnosed. It affects everyone in the family and often extends to loved ones outside the immediate family. Or as my husband once said after he received his third cancer diagnosis, "It's not my cancer; it's our family's cancer." And with it came the temptation to cave in to worry, anxiety, and fear. (As my husband quipped, "Honey, you're an experiential writer. I thought this would give you material for your next book!" Who said I needed more material?)

Sweaty palms, racing pulse, headaches, butterflies in the stomach, difficulty concentrating, feeling overwhelmed—any or all of these symptoms could indicate worry, anxiety, or fear. I've experienced them all and more. I've felt so wrapped up in knots that I wasn't sure I could get out of bed in the morning or that I even wanted to.

Have you ever had any of the following conversations, even if only in your head?

"I can't do ____, because I'm afraid that ____."

"I won't do ____, because I'm worried about ____."

"I'm not sure about ____, because I fear ____ might happen."

If you have, then you have come face-to-face with worry, anxiety, or fear, and you're not alone. Many people experience worry, anxiety, and fear but often view such experiences as an inescapable way of life, as the norm. Worry, anxiety, and fear are considered the common cold of mental illness and are a direct path to losing our peace. "This is what the LORD says: 'Cries of fear are heard—terror, not peace'" (Jer. 30:5).

I can relate; I hated feeling worried, anxious, and afraid with every fiber of my being, but I felt powerless to change my feelings. During a season in my life when my husband was undergoing treatment for cancer and I felt the burden of providing for our family, worry, anxiety, and fear threatened me like a noose around my neck. Every morning my thoughts raced before my eyes opened, a boulder resided in the pit of my stomach, and I cried during my commute to work, feeling powerless to fight back against the feelings that smothered me.

Every week patients come into my office and recount similar descriptions. Some name specific fears, while others share more general worries. But the underlying misery is always the same.

Diane admitted:

> It's mentally and physically exhausting. Mentally, I feel lonely, disconnected, emotionally immature, disappointed in myself, like a failure, and utterly hopeless of ever living a normal life. Physically, anxiety triggered by endless fear causes nervous butterflies in my stomach; a spaced-out feeling; tightness in my chest, neck, and shoulders; and headaches. Sometimes noise seems magnified or my hearing feels impaired, and I have no energy. I live much of my life in fight-or-flight response, fearful of a pending harmful event or threat to survival. I just want to escape it all but don't know how.

Jill explained:

> When anxiety or fear hits, I shake and can't stop moving. I have an inability to focus and experience tunnel vision. I'm on the verge of tears and sense being completely out of control and not knowing what to do.

Ecklund described her experience:

> Anxiety can feel different at different times even to the same person. The same trigger can cause different symptoms on different days. The most common feeling for me is being trapped inside my head, believing people are talking about me or things are out to get me. My heart races and I can't stop it, yet on the outside people can't tell anything is going on. Often I need to stop and sit because I can't put one foot in front of the other. Anxiety robs me of sleep. I fear closing my eyes because I am trapped with my thoughts. Other times I sleep to escape my thoughts. Other times anxiety manifests as procrastination. I worry what I do won't be good enough, so I put things off.

Some of the most common pressure points for worry, anxiety, and fear include jobs (and job loss), loss of financial wherewithal, nighttime (i.e., when the to-do list isn't finished or your head fills with ruminating thoughts), and when things a person depends on for stability or regularity start to come undone (i.e., when the cadence of life gets interrupted).

The likelihood that an individual will not encounter some degree of worry, anxiety, or fear at some time is incredibly small. Standard treatment for worry, anxiety, and fear typically includes medication (anxiolytics, antidepressants, or beta-blockers) and/or psychotherapy (often cognitive-behavioral therapy, which helps people identify and avoid anxiety-producing thoughts). Most books focus on these common treatments. This book also addresses the spiritual component, which must be considered if complete healing is desired.

What Is It?

According to the *Diagnostic and Statistical Manual of Mental Disorders*, "*Fear* is the emotional response to real or perceived imminent threat, whereas *anxiety* is anticipation of future threat. Obviously, these two states overlap, but they also differ, with fear more often associated with surges of autonomic arousal necessary for fight or flight, thoughts of immediate danger, and escape behaviors, and anxiety often associated with muscle tension and vigilance in preparation for future danger and cautious or avoidant behaviors." [1]

We often try to categorize our experience, but essentially, worry, anxiety, and fear are varying levels of the same condition. Worry is at the mild end, then comes anxiety, with fear at the other end. Beyond fear is panic. Because people don't want to admit their struggles, these feelings become the elephant in the room.

Worry

According to Webster, worry means "to think about problems or fears: to feel and show fear or concern because you think that something bad has happened or could happen." [2] Worry is essentially thoughts about an unknown future that create anxious feelings that often camp out in the realm of the catastrophic. While worrying often leads to problem solving, it frequently entails problems that can't yet be solved or don't need solving. Our imaginations work overtime and take us to the dark, negative pockets of our minds. Worry frequently results in overstimulation, helplessness, and an unpredictable outcome.

Anxiety

Webster defines anxiety as "a painful or apprehensive uneasiness of mind usually over an impending or anticipated ill" or "an abnormal and overwhelming sense of apprehension and fear often marked by physiological signs (as sweating, tension, and increased pulse), by doubt concerning the reality and nature of the threat, and by self-doubt about one's capacity to cope with it." [3]

Essentially, we become anxious when we survey our circumstances and our surroundings for potential danger, attempting to obtain certainty in otherwise uncertain conditions in an effort to stay safe and plan for every possible eventuality. Anxiety frequently comes with heightened senses, muscle tension, and feeling on edge. While anxiety may have served our prehistoric ancestors well when noises beyond the cave signaled danger, it holds less value when it pertains to imagining potential future scenarios. Our brains cannot discern between reality and vividly imagined thoughts, so mentally anticipating tragedy leads to apprehension and anxiety.

Typically, anxiety attacks are a response to a specific stressor or worry over a potential danger. For example, an anxiety attack may occur in response to fear of a medical procedure or going to court. During an anxiety attack, a person may experience an increased startle response, muscle tension, shortness of breath, dizziness, an increased pulse rate, sweating, difficulty concentrating, fatigue, or irritability. The symptoms usually intensify over a period of time, don't usually last very long, and typically end as soon as the stressful trigger goes away. In some cases, however, the symptoms associated with more general anxiety may be prolonged, lasting days, weeks, or months.

Anxiety is one of the most prevalent of all mental health disorders.[4] Within the general population, anxiety disorders (including generalized anxiety disorder, panic disorder, post-traumatic stress disorder, separation anxiety disorder, and phobias) are the most common class of mental health disorders.[5] Worldwide, an estimated 7.3 percent of the population suffers from an anxiety disorder, [6] which equates to roughly one out of thirteen people[7] or 264 million individuals.[8]

According to the World Health Organization, anxiety disorders are the sixth largest contributor to global disability.[9] According to the National Institute of Mental Health, anxiety disorders are among the most common mental health disorders within the United States, impacting 40 million US adults or 18 percent of the population.[10] Such disorders come with a high cost to the United States, amounting to over $42 billion annually.[11] While anxiety disorders can be effectively treated, only about one-third of those who suffer receive treatment.[12] Yet "people with an anxiety disorder are three to five times more likely to go to the doctor and six times more likely to be hospitalized for psychiatric disorders than those who do not suffer from anxiety disorders."[13]

Reports suggest that anxiety disorders are more common in women than in men.[14] Compared to males, females are 60 percent more likely to suffer from an anxiety disorder at some point in their lives.[15] Anxiety can occur at any age, although the average age of onset is eleven years old.[16] While the prevalence rates are fairly consistent among age groups, lower prevalence has been suggested in older ages.[17] These statistics refer to *diagnosed* cases; many people do not seek treatment, and many more struggle with subclinical but pervasive anxiety that impacts their quality of life.

In my practice, I am often asked, "Is anxiety a new epidemic, or are people just more comfortable talking about it? Has it always been this prevalent?"

Anxiety has been part of the human experience since Adam and Eve's encounter with the serpent in the garden. It was their unhealthy fear of God that led them to hide once they became aware of their nakedness.

At the same time, we are becoming more aware of anxiety. Children naturally have fears because of their limited experience and greater exposure to adult stressors, difficult circumstances, and anxiety-provoking situations, but the degree to which they are being diagnosed with anxiety has increased, in my experience, over the last decade.

Anxiety frequently accompanies major life stressors, but for many, there is no obviously identifiable trigger. Anxiety often begins small and inconsequential, but left untreated, it often takes on a life of its own and can become incapacitating.

Fear

Webster defines fear as "an unpleasant, often strong emotion caused by anticipation or awareness of danger."[18] Fear is a response to danger or a threat that has yet to occur and engages a fight-or-flight response with physiological changes such as rapid breathing (to receive increased oxygen), increased heartbeat (to deliver oxygenated blood to the muscles that are ready to act because of adrenalin), and sweating (to cool the body), all of which prepare the body to engage in full panic if necessary.

The degree of fear is determined by the seriousness of the threat, how unpleasant the threat is, and how far it is into the future. Prolonged fear is a response to thoughts rather than a real scenario. As a result, fear can be exhausting. Physiologically, the fear response was designed for short-term survival sprints rather than a long-term marathon.

> *Physiologically, the fear response was designed for short-term survival sprints rather than a long-term marathon.*

"There are more than two hundred recognized fears and phobias."[19] Phobias are generally thought of as significant and persistent fears that are considered excessive or unreasonable and last at least six months. The most common fears are fear of the unknown or of the future, change, failure, loss (i.e., of life, loved ones, opportunity), others (i.e., their opinions, ridicule, lack of acceptance, intimacy, rejection, abandonment), hurt (i.e., betrayed trust or being let down), lack of provision or insufficient resources, lack of safety, public speaking, death, success, and God.

Panic

Most people experience anxiety at some point in their lives, but relatively few people actually experience a full-blown panic attack. Anxiety is a response to an anticipated threat that hasn't yet occurred, whereas panic is generally a response to a real and present danger.

Panic is an extension of fear but in an extreme form. It involves being totally overwhelmed by physical and mental feelings. This happens when one is faced with a sudden life-threatening danger at this very moment or has a delayed response to a previously experienced danger. The panic response to a current danger is vital because it gets the body into the optimum state for survival—ready to fight, flee, or sometimes even freeze.

Panic is more often experienced in the context of a panic attack. In a truly dangerous situation, the physical effects of panic are put to good use fighting or fleeing, and the person focuses on doing just that rather than thinking about how they are feeling. Only when panic strikes for no apparent reason does a person have the chance to become aware of its many physical sensations.[20] These include shortness of breath, difficulty breathing, heart palpitations, chest pain, trembling, nausea, intense sweating, chills or hot flashes, and dizziness. The onset of symptoms is generally sudden, without forewarning, and the severity intense. The symptoms appear to "come out of the blue" and may last several minutes.

Unlike anxiety attacks, which are in response to a specific trigger or stressor, panic attacks are unprovoked and unpredictable. During a panic attack, a person experiences an incapacitating feeling of fear and dread. The sudden, overwhelming onset of panic leaves them feeling paralyzed and afraid, sometimes to the point of fearing they might have a heart attack or die. Once someone has experienced a panic attack, they may be prone to anticipatory anxiety (fear of or worry about having another panic attack). Because the fear is so pronounced, they may begin avoiding places they previously experienced a panic attack. Sadly for many, panic attacks leave them feeling overwhelmed, incapacitated, and afraid to leave the house, resulting in withdrawal from activities they previously enjoyed.

Psalm 55:4–5 describes panic fairly well: "My heart is in anguish within me; the terrors of death have fallen on me. Fear and trembling have beset me; horror has overwhelmed me."

We all experience worry and fear at times, but not all experiences lead to a diagnosable anxiety disorder. While some people are diagnosed with specific anxiety disorders (such as generalized anxiety disorder, obsessive compulsive disorder, post-traumatic stress disorder, phobias, social anxiety, and agoraphobia), this book pertains to all varieties and degrees of worry, anxiety, and fear. Regardless of whether one has been diagnosed with an anxiety disorder or lives with daily worries, the end result is a lack of peace.

The Damaging Effects of Worry, Anxiety, and Fear

One of the most recognizable negative effects of worry, anxiety, and fear is the physical toll it takes on the body. The list of physical symptoms is endless. When real or perceived stressors occur, the body prepares to respond: the heart beats faster, muscles tense, breathing quickens, senses become more acute, and hormones are released into the body. If no threat approaches, the body remains on high alert. A person may experience sweating, heart palpitations, light-headedness, nausea, and muscle aches and pains. Excessive worry, anxiety, and fear can have a detrimental impact on both sleep and appetite and can lead to harmful lifestyle habits such as smoking and drinking. Prolonged worry, anxiety, and fear cause excessive amounts of cortisol, the stress hormone, to be released into the body, convincing the brain that a prolonged state of emergency exists. Prolonged or repeated bouts of worry, anxiety, and fear contribute to life-threatening physical ailments such as heart disease, chronic respiratory disease, and diabetes and to other less dangerous but troubling conditions such as fatigue, irritable bowel syndrome, and migraine headaches.

Emotionally, worry, anxiety, and fear can lead to panic attacks and depression. Most of the emotional response is due to stress or perceived stress. Anxiety essentially causes long-term stress on the body. Prolonged stress leads to a change in brain chemicals called neurotransmitters, which contribute to emotional regulation. When experiencing worry, anxiety, or fear, a person tends to anticipate the worst-case scenario. They may feel agitated, restless, jumpy, or tense. They may feel irritable and experience difficulty concentrating. To a large extent, the typical avoidance response to the things that cause worry, anxiety, and fear reinforces further avoidance, because when a person avoids, the anxiety temporarily dissipates. Unfortunately, worry, anxi-

ety, and fear often start over minor concerns, but left untreated, they
can grow to encompass more triggers and become chronic over time.
Worry, anxiety, and fear can also have a detrimental impact on
relationships. They can cause social withdrawal. A person may avoid
interaction with others in settings that trigger heightened worry, anxiety, and fear. Worry, anxiety, and fear can also result in reduced work
efficiency. A person may lie to cover up the real reason tasks did not
get accomplished, and many who experience such emotions become
defensive or suspicious of others. Some also become more impulsive in
their behavior (e.g., smoking, drinking, gambling, impulse buying).

Peace: The Antithesis of Worry, Anxiety, and Fear

In direct opposition to worry, anxiety, and fear is peace. It's physiologically impossible to be relaxed (at peace) and anxious at the same time.
When we entertain worry, anxiety, and fear, we sacrifice our peace.
Sadly, many of us have forfeited our dreams
and our peace because we live in our fears.

For the longest time, I wasn't even sure
I could tell you what peace was, other than
a word in a Christmas carol. When I asked
a group of people to define peace, they offered the following: "absence of worry/
fear," "contented," "a settledness of mind,
body, and spirit," "all is well with my soul
even when my outside circumstances are
in turmoil," "a calm or stillness regardless
of the chaos or quietness of the situation," and my favorite, "Peace is
not the absence of chaos but our response to it. Being at peace means
we can rest, be still, and trust God to keep us safe through it all."

> *It's physiologically
impossible to be relaxed
(at peace) and anxious
at the same time. When
we entertain worry,
anxiety, and fear, we
sacrifice our peace.*

Peace is defined as "a state of tranquility or quiet; freedom from
disquieting or oppressive thoughts or emotions."[21] I've come to
understand peace as an absence of worry, concern, or annoyance, a
calm experience in my mind and my heart. Lao Tzu said, "If you are

depressed, you are living in the past. If you are anxious, you are living in the future. If you are at peace, you are living in the present."[22]

The apostle Paul frequently used the word *peace* in the salutation of his letters. He repeatedly stated, "Grace to you and peace from God our Father and the Lord Jesus Christ." Fear, anxiety, stress, and worry are the enemy's tools to keep us in bondage. But fear is NOT our portion! God desires for us to experience his peace. "Now may the Lord of peace himself give you his peace at all times and in every situation" (2 Thess. 3:16 NLT).

Jill put it this way:

> No one wants to be the victim of worry, anxiety, and fear, yet when people experience them, most feel controlled by them and powerless to change. The good news is that there is hope for living a peace-filled, fearless, worry-free life.

As we journey together toward peace, we will discuss where worry, anxiety, and fear originate. We will take a closer look at how they slip into our daily lives and take up residence. We will discuss the necessity of understanding the spiritual battle that prevents more individuals from experiencing God's peace. And we will examine how God has already given us the tools to effectively exchange our worry, anxiety, and fear for his peace. David Jeremiah said, "The more you fix your eyes on God's purpose for you, the more you will overcome your fear."[23] Are you ready to unload your backpack of worry, anxiety, and fear and walk the path of peace? Then let's get going!

Your Rx

1. Look up the following verses: Psalm 139:23 and 2 Thessalonians 3:16. Then write them on index cards and place them where you will see them frequently. Read each of these passages aloud three times daily, committing them to memory.

2. Reread the descriptions of worry, anxiety, and fear. Ask God to reveal any areas in your life where you struggle with any of them. Then pray, asking him to guide you through the pages of this book to a life of peace.

3. Think about your daily life. In what areas do you desire greater peace? In prayer, commit to following Christ's leading into the peace he came to give.

My Prayer for You

Father, you know that sometimes life and the circumstances we face are just hard. But you are our source of peace. I pray for the one reading these words. I pray that despite what they are facing right now, they will take a deep breath and inhale more of you and your peace while exhaling the worries and fears that weigh them down. I pray that they will be anxious for no thing and will go to you in prayer with all their needs, thanking you even now that you know how you're going to care for every last detail. Thank you that you care about the things we care about and that you are our source of peace in the midst of the storms. In Jesus's name, amen.

Recommended Playlist

"Fear Is a Liar," Zach Williams, © 2016 by Provident Label Group LLC

"Peace in Christ," McKenna Hixson, © 2017 by Intellectual Reserve, Inc.

"Surrounded (Fight My Battles)," Michael W. Smith, © 2017 by Rocketown Records / The Fuel Music

"Good Life," The Young Escape, © 2017 by Sparrow Records

"The Breakup Song," Francesca Battistelli, © 2018 by Word Entertainment LLC

2

Why Me?

For God hath not given us the spirit of fear; but of power, and of love, and of a sound mind.

2 Timothy 1:7 KJV

Worry implies that we don't quite trust that God is big enough, powerful enough, or loving enough to take care of what's happening in our lives.

Francis Chan

The Thief of Peace

They stepped in like a thief in the night and stole from me, and stole from my family.

Has that ever happened to you? Things were going well, and then it happened—"it" being worry, anxiety, and fear. Almost like I'd given them a key to my front door, worry, anxiety, and fear let themselves in without even asking.

Actually, I did give them permission. I listened to them, entertained them, agreed with them, and let them stay. I didn't catch their suave entrance or tell them to leave.

"What makes you think people want to hear what you have to say?"

"What would they say if they knew you aren't perfect?"

"If you don't take care of it, no one will."

"If God cared, he would've answered your prayers by now."

Worry, anxiety, and fear are insidious. They creep in like a weekend guest and then take on a life of their own, moving in for the long haul before you even realize what happened.

But in gaining entrance to my mind and heart, they stole from me. Worry stole my joy. Anxiety stole my peace. Fear stole my present as it projected into my future. And they stole from my family because I couldn't be truly present with them when I was worried about the past or the future.

Debbie explained her experience this way:

> I experienced overwhelming thoughts of worry, anxiety, and fear—the trifecta of all three—as I worked through the process of writing and launching my first traditionally published book. It began with a thought, then I worried I wasn't enough. My thoughts raced, then got carried away like a runaway train, turning into fear and anxiety. I was overwhelmed and discouraged, and even though I knew the truth in God's Word, my feelings threatened to overtake me. It was a full-on assault designed to take me out.

Our Chief Anxiety

In the Sermon on the Mount, Jesus instructs us not to worry (Matt. 6:25–34). He specifically calls out worry about what we'll eat or drink or what we'll wear. In the middle of this exposition, Jesus states that such things are what most of the world "runs after" (v. 32). He puts his finger on our chief anxiety: How will I be provided for tomorrow?

Many have no sense of how this question gets answered other than by their own sweat and blood. It involves reaching and striving and working more, or more intensely, because they think they must. Perhaps it involves cheating or stealing from another, either explicitly or implicitly.

We expend mental energy attempting to answer this question. We rail against scenarios in which the answer to the question isn't what we want. We try to find a solution to each of the worries that may not even happen. The potentials are endless, and none of the thoughts or plans or what-ifs can be acted on because the calamitous events that we fearfully construct in our minds haven't occurred. So we sit and brood, waiting for the worst to happen, for our lives to be slowly deconstructed in one area or another.

Jesus's counter to this is our heavenly Father, the Author of life and the Creator of each individual, who knows our needs and desires. The Creator of the human body won't let it go hungry or unclothed; it's more precious to him than the rest of creation. Jesus instructs us to seek relationship with our Father first, and then all other things will fall into a proper perspective.

Jesus ends his sermon with a couple wry observations. He states that tomorrow will worry about its own things, so we shouldn't worry about them now. We are not at tomorrow yet! We are at today, and Jesus closes by saying, "Sufficient for the day is its own trouble" (Matt. 6:34 NKJV). We should take care of what we need to do today, but we shouldn't be concerned about what tomorrow will bring. God is at tomorrow; we are not.

The Birth of Worry, Anxiety, and Fear

Those in the medical community generally talk about three primary contributors to worry, anxiety, and fear: brain chemistry, heredity, and life experiences. In truth, much isn't known about the origin of anxiety disorders, and there's rarely a simple answer to "Where did it come from?" Often by the time someone seeks medical attention for worry, anxiety, or fear, they no longer remember what was happening when they first experienced symptoms.

Sometimes a more important question than "Why?" or "Where did it come from?" is "What can I do about it?" We'll get to that question later, but first let's spend a few moments looking at the contributors to worry, anxiety, and fear.

Brain Chemistry

Our brains are equipped with special chemicals called neurotransmitters that help regulate functions such as mood, motivation, sleep, and appetite. These neurotransmitters help pass information from one part of the brain to another. Examples of such chemicals are dopamine, gamma-aminobutyric acid (GABA), norepinephrine, and serotonin.

Dysregulation of these neurotransmitters (too much or too little) can contribute to symptoms of anxiety. Depending on the amount of each of these chemicals in the brain, different symptoms of anxiety may surface, such as feeling jittery or nervous, having difficulty sleeping, sweating, and so on. Individuals can take medication in an effort to regulate these neurotransmitters in hopes of reducing or eliminating the symptoms related to worry, anxiety, and fear. Medicines that regulate neurotransmitters can be powerful aids, but they only treat symptoms. They do not cure anxiety, just as aspirin does not heal a sprained ankle. Aspirin reduces the pain from a sprained ankle, but when the medicine wears off, the pain returns. In the same way, medicines for anxiety only treat symptoms but not the underlying causes.

Heredity

Another contributor to worry, anxiety, and fear is heredity. Just as many sufferers of heart disease, cancer, diabetes, or dementia may have a genetic predisposition to these conditions, so others may have a genetic predisposition to worry, anxiety, and fear. Those who suffer can often look back into their ancestry and identify others in their family tree who exhibited signs or symptoms, even if they did not have a full-blown diagnosable anxiety disorder. Not everyone with anxiety-prone relatives will succumb to worry, anxiety, or fear, but there is an increased likelihood. Furthermore, early life experience of anxiety increases the likelihood that an anxiety disorder will be diagnosed later.

Life Experiences

MODELING

A compounding contributor to heredity is the fact that when a close relative struggles with worry, anxiety, or fear, they tend to model the related symptoms, tendencies, and mind-sets in the home. A mother who worries that her children may not be safe within the home or walking to school or shopping in a mall may inadvertently model her fear for her children, which in turn teaches them to be fearful and apprehensive.

OUR THOUGHTS

Differing amounts of neurotransmitters in the brain contribute to symptoms of anxiety, and research has shown that our thoughts impact the production of neurotransmitters. While brain chemistry can impact mood and behavior, thoughts (e.g., "This place isn't safe," "I can't handle this anymore," "I'm overwhelmed," etc.) actually impact brain chemistry.

This is precisely why we must pay attention to the thoughts we allow into our minds. Scripture encourages, "Set your minds on things above, not on earthly things" (Col. 3:2). If we focus on our pain or our difficulties rather than on God, we open ourselves up to worry, anxiety, and fear. On the other hand, if we focus our thoughts on God rather than our circumstances, we can maintain our peace.

THE HEART

While neurochemistry and genetics may contribute to worry, anxiety, and fear, Scripture speaks to the importance of guarding the heart. "Guard your heart above all else, for it determines the course of your life" (Prov. 4:23 NLT). When we watch disturbing footage on television or read frightening stories on the internet rather than guarding our hearts from things we can't unsee or unhear, we allow our hearts to be infiltrated by anxiety-provoking messages.

Scripture says, "For whatever is in your heart determines what you say" (Matt. 12:34 NLT). When we allow our hearts to be penetrated by fear-inducing stories and messages, we then speak from worry, anxiety, and fear. This in turn exacerbates our own anxiety as well as pushes it out to be consumed by our listeners.

When my husband was first diagnosed with cancer, we chose, as much as possible, not to view the evening news or to read sensational newspaper headlines that would bring us down or invoke anxiety. We wanted our hearts focused on the positive, encouraging aspects of life, consistent with Philippians 4:8: "Whatever is true, whatever is noble, whatever is right, whatever is pure, whatever is lovely, whatever is admirable—if anything is excellent or praiseworthy—think about such things." We did this not only for ourselves but also for our children.

Guarding our hearts also meant being careful with whom we chose to share our concerns. When I endured a fourteen-week bout of pneumonia and when my husband was diagnosed with cancer, some people thought it was important to share how their father's uncle's friend had died from such conditions. People often do not recognize how their words can instill fear.

Spiritual Roots

While we must consider the physical, cognitive, and emotional components of worry, anxiety, and fear, we cannot ignore the spiritual component if we desire healing and freedom from anxiety's chains. In his Word, God clearly reveals the root of worry, anxiety, and fear. "For God hath not given us *the spirit of fear*; but of power, and of love, and of a sound mind" (2 Tim. 1:7 KJV, emphasis added). As much as we may not like to think about this aspect, Scripture is clear: "For our struggle is not against flesh and blood, but against the rulers, against the authorities, against the powers of this dark world and against the spiritual forces of evil in the heavenly realms" (Eph. 6:12).

We have a very real enemy, and our fear of him only enhances his power. He wants us to believe we are slaves to our past, our mistakes, even worry, anxiety, and fear. Fear keeps us from stepping into our God-given calling. It tells us we aren't capable. Fear projects past failures, hurts, and rejection into our future to keep us stuck. Fear makes excuses and is based on a lie.

Satan's fall from heaven resulted from his desire for control. He desired to be greater than God and to be in control (Isa. 14:12–16). Largely, our experience of worry, anxiety, and fear results from a similar desire and our inability to be in control of all aspects of our lives. We worry when we are stuck in traffic on the way to an important meeting, not wanting to be late but powerless to control the roadways. We become anxious when life-threatening diagnoses are rendered by doctors, even though we are unable to control how our bodies have failed us. We become fearful when forecasters predict catastrophic events such as tornadoes and hurricanes, even though we are unable to do anything about their path or the destruction that may ensue.

Peace comes from living in the present and remembering what has already been accomplished in the past to assure us of our future.

Little has changed since the Garden of Eden. God remains in control, yet we wrestle with our desire to control on a daily basis.

Ultimately, fear results from believing the enemy's lies and considering the future, a future in which we feel we must provide for ourselves rather than rely on God's provision. God tells us not to worry about the future because each day has enough problems of its own. Worrying about the future robs us of the joy of the present. It also focuses our attention on the problem, not the Problem Solver!

While we can consider the future, we need not spend too much time there. Instead, we can focus on God's presence, which is with us in the moment and has already gone before us. Attuning our minds to his presence gives us confident peace. In his Word, he promises to make the way of the righteous smooth (Isa. 26:7). Peace comes from living in the present and remembering what has already been accomplished in the past to assure us of our future.

Do You Ever Struggle to Trust God?

Let me be the first to admit that I struggle with trusting God. Oh, I may not call it such, but when I fear, I'm not trusting that God is capable of handling a situation. When I strive in my own strength to make things happen, I'm not trusting his ultimate provision. Sometimes I'm prone to believe that God will answer a friend's prayer but not mine, which points to a lack of trust in him because the Bible says he does not play favorites (Acts 10:34).

Difficulty trusting God has been a problem since the beginning. If we go back to the Garden of Eden, we see the first woman who struggled to trust God. She was the mother of all humanity, a friend of God who walked and talked with him daily in the garden. He supplied her every need, and yet she didn't trust him. She fell prey to the serpent, who tempted her with the very thing she wanted but already had. She wanted to be more like God, but she was already like God. He created her in his image.

If Eve had trusted God, trusted that he was good, that he would provide for her every need, and that he loved her enough not to withhold any good gift from her, she would not have listened to and believed the enemy's lies. She would not have searched elsewhere.

How often do we search elsewhere for the things we desire? The things we think we need? The things God has already given us? Such as peace.

- I looked to people for wisdom, when God promises he liberally gives wisdom to whoever asks for it.

- I went through independent streaks, trying to prove my strength, when he promises to be our strength.
- I worried about providing for my family, when God promises to be our provider.
- I looked to people for acceptance, when God says he loves and accepts us unconditionally and that his love will never fail us.

Eve suffered consequences for her misplaced trust, just as we experience consequences when we don't trust God. Our mistrust, like hers, results in a fractured relationship with the very God who created us and loves us perfectly. Placing our faith or trust in the lies of the enemy results in emptiness; nothing he offers ever satisfies. Believing the enemy results in worry, anxiety, and fear. Yet if we trust God, he promises to meet our needs (Phil. 4:19).

> *We tend to approach life thinking,* Show me, then I'll trust you, *but God tells us to trust him, and then he'll show us.*

Worry ends when we enact our faith. The one fundamental thing that God asks from us is that we believe, that we trust him. "And without faith it is impossible to please God, because anyone who comes to him must believe that he exists and that he rewards those who earnestly seek him" (Heb. 11:6). We tend to approach life thinking, *Show me, then I'll trust you*, but God tells us to trust him, and then he'll show us.

God is worthy of our trust.

Heather shared:

> I grew up with the spirit of fear from adolescence until after I married. I was afraid of going out in the dark, even in my own yard. I was terrified and just couldn't do it. I lay many nights in my bedroom with the covers over my head, praying under my breath, asking God to protect me. Sometimes I could only say Jesus's name with my eyes shut so tight I thought my head would explode. Daytime wasn't bad, but I dreaded the setting sun.

> I felt shame thinking my friends would discover how scared I was as a young adult. In college, I feared my own shadow. I hated going to the dorm alone at night, afraid something was waiting to jump out at me. Besides my family, my husband was the only one who knew how afraid I was. In a new city, I felt afraid while he worked nights as an officer. I counted the minutes until he arrived home. I felt safe only in someone else's presence. If just one person was with me, then I felt fine. I always had someone with me, the Spirit of the living God, but I still lived in fear. It was a bondage that entangled me too long. Fear enslaved me, and I let the spirit of fear reign in my mind and my heart.

Freedom Is a Process

As God walked with me in my journey to relinquish worry, anxiety, and fear, he showed me that exchanging them for his peace isn't a onetime event. It's a process. I'm grateful that the book of Psalms gives us a glimpse of David's struggle, a bit like spiritual whiplash. In one breath, he laments about his worries and fears, and in the next, he returns to profess his faith in God, who reigns bigger than all his fears.

While we will discuss the process of gaining freedom from worry, anxiety, and fear throughout the pages of this book, we begin with the clues Jeremiah gives us for exchanging our worries, anxieties, and fears for God's peace: "Blessed is the man who trusts in the LORD, whose trust is the LORD. He is like a tree planted by water, that sends out its roots by the stream, and does not fear when heat comes, for its leaves remain green, and is not anxious in the year of drought, for it does not cease to bear fruit" (Jer. 17:7–8 ESV).

T-R-U-S-T God

Ridding ourselves of worry, anxiety, and fear requires that we trust God. Worry is really a misappropriation of our trust, giving it to a counterfeit that never satisfies. Trusting God, however, brings a sweet, satisfying peace.

In many respects, this book could've been titled *Trust Prevails*, because to live in peace, we must first trust God. The Bible repeatedly encourages that if we trust in the Lord, we will not be disappointed (Ps. 25:3; Isa. 49:23; Rom. 10:11; 1 Pet. 2:6). What an empowering promise.

My attempts to fully trust God have been a tug-of-war. Sometimes I trust him so easily. Other times I fight with all my might trying to achieve in my own strength rather than trusting his. God isn't interested in fighting a battle to persuade us to trust him. He gave all the reasons in his Word for us to trust him. Now he patiently waits for us to respond. Sometimes we quickly agree with his Word, while other times we learn the hard way. Given his promise that we won't be disappointed when we trust him, let's endeavor to trust him without reservation.

The following are "Five Keys to Trusting God," coinciding with the letters T-R-U-S-T.

T—TAKE GOD AT HIS WORD

To trust God, we must believe that God will not lie or break his promises. Sometimes trusting is difficult because we've been let down by people we trusted. People make promises but don't always follow through. In our disappointment, our willingness to trust becomes fractured. But God assures us that he is not like us. He cannot lie and always keeps his Word. "God is not like people, who lie; he is not a human who changes his mind. Whatever he promises, he does; he speaks, and it is done" (Num. 23:19 GNT).

R—REST IN HIS PRESENCE

The dictionary defines *rest* as "refreshing ease or inactivity after exertion or labor" or "to relieve weariness by cessation of exertion or labor."[1] The Hebrew word for rest is *nuach*—to rest, to be quiet. Resting in God's presence reflects our knowledge that we are safe with him and that he will work for our good and for his glory. Resting in his presence means that instead of ruminating on our burdens (unconfessed sin, worry, anxiety, fear, low self-esteem, feelings of shame, etc.) and letting them weigh us down and steal our peace, we ask Jesus to carry them. Jesus said, "Come to me, all you who are weary and burdened, and I will give you rest. Take my yoke upon you and learn from me, for I am gentle and humble in heart, and you will find rest for your souls. For my yoke is easy and my burden is light" (Matt. 11:28–30).

In order to receive God's rest, we must first come to him by praying, reading his Word, worshiping, and repenting, knowing that we are safe in his care. God doesn't withdraw from us; rather, we withdraw from him. When our heart is clean before God, he quiets our soul and we can truly enter his rest. "I have calmed and quieted myself" (Ps. 131:2).

"Whoever dwells in the shelter of the Most High will rest in the shadow of the Almighty" (Ps. 91:1). God calls us not to just come visit him like a hotel guest but to live with him and seek to know him, his heart, and his wisdom. It's a conscious decision to rest in God's promises, to believe he is sufficient, and to trust not only that he is who he says he is but also that he will fulfill his promises to us.

U—UNDERSTAND THE OUTCOME DOESN'T DEPEND ON US

Trusting God means acknowledging that he is in control. We can remain content in that knowledge rather than striving in our own strength. When we trust God, we relinquish control while telling God, "I believe your way is best—whatever that may be." Trusting God takes the responsibility for the outcome off our shoulders and places it on God's. That brings peace because our vision in any situation is limited to what we know about the past and the present. But God knows all things past, present, and future. There is no limit to his knowledge, for God knows everything completely before it even happens (Rom. 11:33).

When we trust God, we relinquish control and acknowledge God's way is best—whatever that may be. Our understanding of ourselves, others, and all situations is limited, so we can't rely on our own understanding. We can, however, confidently trust that God knows all things—including the outcome of any situation. "Lean on, trust in, and be confident in the Lord with all your heart and mind and do not rely on your own insight or understanding" (Prov. 3:5 AMPC).

Trusting God takes the responsibility for the outcome off our shoulders and places it on God's.

As we trust God, we believe even on the hard days, even in the challenges when we don't see the resolution that God can turn our messes into something good. "For those who love God all things work together for good" (Rom. 8:28 ESV). The outcome depends on God, not us.

S—ACCEPT GOD IS SOVEREIGN

In accepting God's sovereignty, we agree that he is the supreme source of all power and authority. Whereas we struggle with many things, nothing is too difficult for him. God can do and accomplish all things. Whatever he wants to do in the universe, he does. Nothing is impossible with him (Jer. 32:17).

When we accept God's sovereignty, recognize that he is in control, and remember that he works all things together for our good and for his glory, we can trust that there is a purpose in our situation and that we aren't alone in the battle. Our worry, anxiety, and fear come largely from feeling out of control, but because God is sovereign, we can trust that he is in control and that he never withholds good from his children (Ps. 84:11).

T—TURN TO THE TESTIMONY OF PREVIOUS EXPERIENCES

In times when our trust wanes, others' testimonies about what God has done in their lives can encourage us. We can also recall our own past experiences when God worked in our lives. We must dwell on his past faithfulness and be confident that there is no reason to doubt him now. "They triumphed over [Satan] by the blood of the Lamb and by the word of their testimony" (Rev. 12:11).

Prepare

Just like a tree planted by water that sends out its roots by the stream, we, too, must prepare. The best way to prepare to fight worry, anxiety, and fear is to learn God's Word and plant it firmly in our hearts. Then we must take our thoughts captive and discern if they are from God or from the enemy. When they're from the enemy, we must exchange them for God's truth. "We destroy arguments and every lofty opinion raised against the knowledge of God, and take every thought captive to obey Christ" (2 Cor. 10:5 ESV).

Many people have asked me how they can determine if their thoughts are from God or from the enemy. Here are some suggestions:

- When God speaks, he never contradicts the Bible or his character. That is why it's so important to know what the Bible says.
- God never condemns or shames us like the enemy does. God forgives us, and his voice gently corrects us out of love, to keep us in a right relationship with him.
- God leads us and stills us, whereas the enemy pushes and rushes us.
- God's voice is comforting, calming, and reassuring, while the enemy worries, frightens, and stresses us.
- While the enemy confuses, God encourages. God is never the author of confusion (1 Cor. 14:33).

Shift the Responsibility

To gain freedom from worry, anxiety, and fear, we must shift the responsibility for all outcomes to God. We must choose not to be anxious but to keep our peace by trusting that just as God causes the leaves to remain green and a crop to grow, so he will help us fulfill whatever he asks of us. I frequently have to remind myself out loud, "Whatever he asks us to do, he equips us through!" When it comes to keeping our peace rather than letting our hearts become troubled or anxious, we have a choice to make: choose to trust in God's powerful and loving provision or try to do it ourselves.

God Will Return What Was Lost

The enemy has stolen many things from us. The good news is that God promises to return everything he has stolen! "The LORD says, 'I will give you back what you lost'" (Joel 2:25 NLT). That includes our peace.

Lucretia said this about her experience with fear:

> Fear was my companion for over five decades. It started out small, like not riding my bike too far or not swimming far into the deep end. My mother parented us out of fear, and her fears became mine. My fears grew during adulthood. I did not take jobs due to a fear of failure, I chose husbands who were not good for me, and I feared being alone or unable to care for myself. I suffered not only from anxiety but also from phobias. I secretly checked locks once, twice, three times. The day of realization came when I arrived at a restaurant, and, after being seated, as I had done many times before, I methodically repositioned everything on the table. I had never realized I'd done it until my companion brought it to my attention. That is when I determined to get help.
>
> I now know that the spirit of fear and his helpers were affecting me (2 Tim. 1:7). Knowing I could do something about my fear brought me freedom. I heard from therapists that I needed to learn how to manage my fear, but I couldn't find the word *manage* anywhere in God's Word. Instead, I learned to take the authority God gave me, through his Holy Spirit.

I love the thought of infuriating the enemy—he has stolen too much from us! The best punishment for the enemy is to relinquish worry, anxiety, and fear and move forward living in peace. Living in peace infuriates the enemy because he possesses no peace.

As we journey together through the following chapters, we will take a deeper look at where and why worry, anxiety, and fear surface. Then we will crush the enemy as we seek together to exchange our worry, anxiety, and fear for the peace Jesus came to give us. "The God of peace will soon crush Satan under your feet. The grace of our Lord Jesus be with you" (Rom. 16:20).

Your Rx

1. Look up the following verses: Joel 2:25; Romans 16:20; Ephesians 6:12; and 2 Timothy 1:7. Then write them on index cards and place them where you will see them frequently. Read each of these passages aloud three times daily, committing them to memory.

2. Read Matthew 6:25–34, where Jesus cautions against worry regarding daily provision. Reread it and take note of what stands out for you. Confess in writing to God those areas he revealed that you tend to worry about. Ask him, in faith, to help you exchange your worry for trust in his provision.

3. Review the three steps under "Freedom Is a Process." Prayerfully consider which is most difficult for you. Ask God to help you in the process. Determine one thing you will do to make forward movement in the process.

My Prayer for You

Father, I thank you that you have not given us the spirit of fear but instead power, love, and a sound mind. Thank you that fear is not our portion but merely deception from the enemy of our souls.

Help each of us to trust you more, prepare, and wait on you for the harvest of peace that you desire for us. Reveal to us the lies we have believed and how to counter them with your truth. In Jesus's name, amen.

Recommended Playlist

"Not Today," Hillsong United, © 2017 by Sparrow Records

"Linger," Gateway Music, © 2018 by Gateway Music

"Mercy," Casting Crowns, © 2011 by Integrity Music

"We Will Not Be Shaken," Bethel Music and Brian Johnson, © 2015 by Bethel Music

"You Are My Hope," Cory Asbury, © 2008 by Forerunner Music

"Fall," The Belonging Co., © 2017 by TBCO Music

3

Fear Lurks

So be on your guard, not asleep like the others. Stay alert and be clearheaded.

1 Thessalonians 5:6 NLT

There is great beauty in going through life without anxiety or fear. Half our fears are baseless and the other half discreditable.

Christian Nestell Bovee

We need only turn on the evening news or scroll through our social media feeds to see where the potential for fear lurks. From natural disasters to economic decline, political unrest to homegrown terrorism, our world provides many opportunities to fear. Even closer to home, we face daily trials and circumstances where fear lurks, ready to assault our very core.

Katelyn's fears left her almost paralyzed:

> Every night for over a year, I panicked when the kids were in bed and I could've relaxed. Physically, my body tingled, and my stomach ached. Sometimes I woke up after the little

sleep I could get, shook, vomited, and had diarrhea. Mentally, my mind raced, considering everything that could go wrong in my life or in the lives of my family members. Thoughts of imagined doom constantly assailed me.

Later, I experienced constant fear and panic. When away from home, I irrationally feared that someone had broken in or the house had burned down. I feared traveling with my husband or taking our kids to functions, afraid we would be killed after dropping them off and fearing what would become of them. I now know I stopped trusting God. I loved him and prayed constantly but did not trust him. Once I discovered that, God took me out of the anxious pit I had dug for myself.

I recently asked a group of people to share what stirs up fear in them. Responses were widespread. Financial loss or ruin was a top fear. Others feared losing loved ones. Some voiced fear concerning aging or health issues. The safety and well-being of children was another common fear.

While there are countless things that can precipitate fear, they generally fall within five basic categories.[1]

1. *Fear of extinction* is a fear of death and all things contributing to our lack of existence. Examples include a fear of heights, flying, and cancer.

2. *Fear of mutilation* entails anything that could threaten the integrity of any part of our bodies or their function. A fear of sharp objects, fire, animals, or insects falls in this realm.

3. *Fear of loss of autonomy* describes fear arising from anticipation of losing control of our circumstances, physically (think claustrophobia) or in relationships. A fear of financial ruin, kidnapping, or paralysis falls within this category.

4. *Fear of separation* generally arises from concern that we will no longer be valued or included in relationships. Examples include a fear of rejection, abandonment, and exclusion.

5. *Fear of ego death* (i.e., humiliation or shame) results from believing we will be humiliated, shamed, or found unlovable or unworthy. The common fears of public speaking, bullying, and not being chosen for that important club or group are all examples.

It's easy to see how fear lurks everywhere in our lives. It waits to take hold of our hearts and minds and paralyze us to the point of immobility. When we learn to identify fear for what it is, we can see where we are vulnerable and learn how to fight back in order to regain the peace that Jesus promised in John 14:27.

Fear: A Self-Fulfilling Prophecy?

My first vivid memory of being afraid comes from early childhood. I lived across a busy street from a large multi-building apartment complex. One fall evening after sunset, our family was eating dinner together when sirens blared. The noise outside escalated until it overcame our chatter. My father rose from the table and looked out our front door. He stood motionless for what seemed like minutes.

When we learn to identify fear for what it is, we can see where we are vulnerable and learn how to fight back in order to regain the peace that Jesus promised.

I peered at him over the back of my dining room chair. "What is it, Daddy?" He remained silent. I hopped down from my seat and ran to his side even as my mother beckoned me to return to my meal. As I stood next to him staring across the street, I wrapped my arms around his leg in fear and trepidation as I watched the apartment complex engulfed in flames. I cried and screamed in terror, afraid the fire would cross the street and threaten our house also.

Firefighters controlled the blaze. It never encroached on our side of the street, but the image of the raging fire and the devastation it caused lingered in my mind for decades. I didn't even learn to light a match until I was in my twenties and married. In some ways, fear of a perceived threat ruled aspects of my life.

Ralph Waldo Emerson said, "Fear defeats more people than any other one thing in the world."[2] I think he was right. When the enemy invokes the spirit of fear, he kills our peace and paralyzes our initiative. Fear immobilizes us, often before we even get started. I experienced this phenomenon when I started writing this book. Many readers of my first book, *Hope Prevails: Insights from a Doctor's Personal Journey through Depression*,[3] commented that it was like I read their mind. I felt such great pressure to offer helpful insights in this book that I literally couldn't get started! Naguib Mahfouz, an Egyptian writer who won the 1988 Nobel Prize for Literature, said, "Fear does not prevent death; it prevents life."[4] That's exactly what fear was doing to me. It was preventing me from doing something productive that I normally enjoy: crafting words to encourage and inspire.

When we allow the spirit of fear to operate in our lives, it is like we are putting a cast on an arm or a leg that doesn't need it. We are allowing it to immobilize us and hinder us from effectively living in the center of the peace that God has offered us. We are not alone in our struggle. Scripture gives examples of biblical greats who also struggled with fear.

Consider Job. He was devoted to God and hated evil. His children loved to have parties, and every morning after their parties, Job sacrificed burnt offerings on their behalf in case they had sinned. Satan scoffed at his integrity and sought to prove to God that Job was not all God thought he was. Through Satan's doing, all of Job's livestock and shepherds were killed, his children were killed when a great wind leveled his son's house, and Job was struck with painful sores over his entire body. "*What I feared* has come upon me; *what I dreaded* has happened to me. I have no peace, no quietness; I have no rest, but only turmoil" (Job 3:25–26, emphasis added). Job's fear and dread amplified his disquiet. The personal picture of disaster that Job had held in his heart made it easy for him to paint himself into the picture frame when that sequence of events came to pass.

Scripture repeatedly commands, "Do not be afraid," "Do not fear," "Do not worry," and "Be anxious for nothing." Ephesians 6:12 says, "For our struggle is not against flesh and blood, but against the rulers, against the authorities, against the powers of this dark world and against the spiritual forces of evil in the heavenly realms." Furthermore, according to 2 Timothy 1:7, we must guard against the spirit of fear: "For God hath not given us the spirit of fear; but of power, and of love, and of a sound mind" (KJV). Job's devastating situation underscores a crucial truth that is key if we want to dispense with worry, anxiety, and fear and remain in God's peace: our thoughts have power. The enemy ushers havoc and trials into our lives when we cooperate with the spirit of fear and agree with him instead of with God's truth.

Job 3:25–26 records that Job had allowed the spirit of fear to influence his thinking, and what he most feared later happened. Once he experienced what he dreaded, he had no peace and no rest but only turmoil.

Have you ever experienced the thing you feared most? We spend much time mulling over our worries, fears, and anxieties even though most never happen. We let the enemy have his way in our lives when we give in to the temptation to worry or fear rather than trust God and allow his peace to permeate our lives. Satan studies our attitudes, behaviors, and words, and learns our individual weaknesses. When we fear or worry about something, we are more likely to look for evidence to confirm we have reason to fear. We might compare our fear to a radio receiver that is tuned to music we dislike or a combative talk show. Of all the possible radio signals, it's the bad stuff we're tuned to. The enemy knows our "frequency." He knows what will get us. We must intentionally turn off the radio or tune it to a positive signal.

As a young teenager, I spent the summer away from home with my mother having reconstructive surgery on a leg and foot deformity the result of a childhood illness. At summer's end, we drove through the night to return home in time for my brother's birthday dinner. We made the dinner, but at three the next morning, my mother woke my brother and me and took us downstairs, where we were greeted in the dark of night by our pastor and his wife. My parents often helped plant churches, so prayer meetings at unusual times and places were the norm for my family. But still I wondered, *What couldn't wait until morning?*

Just then I heard sirens and saw flashing lights as the ambulance reached our home. My mother explained, "Honey, your dad died."

I can't tell you what else was said at that moment, but my first thought was *How can I help my family financially?* My mother was from another country and not a US citizen, and she did not have a formal education or trade. As the oldest child, I felt responsible to help support the family. My next thought was *This will never happen to me. If anything ever happens to my future husband, I will be able to support my family.*

My father's death immediately instilled in me a deep fear that something would eventually happen to my future husband. Rather than seeing my father's death as a passing although significant event and trusting God to provide, I let fear govern my life and dictate my actions and emotions. I allowed the spirit of fear to control me. Approximately a decade later, just like with Job, what I feared came upon me when my husband received a cancer diagnosis with a poor prognosis. I remember recounting my situation to God in prayer: "God you *knew* that I feared this happening more than anything else. You could have stopped this. You could have prevented it. You could have protected me and him."

The truth is, yes, God could have prevented the cancer. But God doesn't promise that we won't experience difficult circumstances. Yet, we don't have to let fear and grief consume us. We can lean on God and his understanding and choose to live in his peace rather than live in worry, anxiety, and fear as Satan would have us do.

We must remember that Job continued to praise God despite the tragedy and loss. Even when he despaired and asked God, "Why?" God blessed Job's later years even more than his earlier years and gave him twice what he had lost (Job 42:10). God understands our humanness. He's looking for an attitude of humility, a willingness to trust him despite how difficult our circumstances appear, and a faith that says, "You are God and I am not, so I will trust in you."

Fear Overrides Logic and Reason

I bolted upright in bed during the charcoal black night, drenched in sweat and gasping for air. The harder I tried to catch my breath, the harder it was to breathe. Fear grabbed me by the throat and strangled every ounce of logic and reason from my mind. Emotions overruled logic. Pure panic set in. As a neuropsychologist, I repeatedly teach my patients that it is physiologically impossible to be relaxed and fearful at the same time. When fear dominates, unhealthy emotions rule, while logic and reason drift away like a balloon slipping from our grasp on a windy day.

Several weeks prior, an irritating cough had worsened, and the accompanying tightness in my chest, heavy weight on my back, and notable fever had prompted an emergency room visit. Lab work and X-rays confirmed the doctor's suspicion: pneumonia. Weeks later, on my third visit to the doctor, she added diagnoses of the flu and bronchitis. I didn't care what diagnosis she offered. I just wanted to breathe without difficulty and not suffer the random frightening bouts of labored breathing that required a rescue inhaler.

My mother had suffered from lung cancer a few years prior and passed away from a related choking event. As I bolted upright drenched in sweat, gasping for air, I thought, *I'm going to die from suffocation!* Nothing frightened me more. Those thoughts brought panic, making it harder to breathe. I dialed a friend to ask her to pray, though I was unable to utter a word, only cough or gasp for air into the receiver. I couldn't think clearly enough to pray for myself, so I relied on others' prayers to wage battle with me. As we wage war against the spirit of fear, sometimes we need to enlist the reinforcement of others to agree with us in our fight.

Fight Back against the Spirit of Fear

Scripture repeatedly commands, "Fear not," "Do not be afraid," and "Be anxious for nothing." I suspect God repeated those commands because he knew how frequently we would struggle and that we would need the reminder not to travel that path. Many books that discuss worry, anxiety, and fear, even from a Christian standpoint, basically say, "God said don't do it, so don't." If not worrying were that easy, I doubt God would have repeated himself so frequently. Few books explain how to combat our tendency to lapse into worry, anxiety, and fear and how to stop the ensuing downhill spiral. I recently got to see this fight against worry, anxiety, and fear happen within my own family.

Toward semester's end, my college-age son texted me, "You free?"

He often jokes with us and brings about many a family chuckle, so I frequently respond in kind. I teased, "No, I'm very expensive!" punctuated with a smiley emoji.

Within seconds, he replied, "No, really."

I knew then that something significant weighed on his mind. "I'm available. Do you need to talk?" I offered.

"Yes. Call you in a few minutes."

I waited, hypothesizing, until the caller ID revealed his number on my phone.

"Mom, I'm really nervous about this exam."

"A little nervousness is okay. It prompts you to prepare, to study, and to do your due diligence."

Truthfully, I remembered feeling exactly the same way two decades prior as I prepared for my board certification. The examination process was comprised of several components, and examinees typically failed at least one. Before the written and oral examinations, my fear was rampant. I couldn't eat, sleep, or think clearly, making it impossible to study effectively. I didn't know how to combat fear then, but I now knew my son needed to claim and hold on to the hope and peace that is already ours in Christ.

As he continued to explain, I was pulled back from my memories to his present predicament. "I just found out about this exam today. I'm more than a little nervous, Mom. I'm jittery, jumping out of my skin, nauseous, and I can't think clearly. I'm almost panicking. I feel overwhelmed."

"You're right, hon, that's more than a little nervousness. That's the spirit of fear."

"What do I do about it?"

"Fear cripples, but God's truth sets us free. Talk back to it! Fear isn't consistent with what your heavenly Father says. You have the mind of Christ, and the Holy Spirit dwells within you. The Holy Spirit's job is to remind you of all truth, and you have studied truth."

He followed along. "Okaaaay . . ."

Fear cripples, but God's truth sets us free.

"When you start to panic or fear, tell the spirit of fear, 'No!' Then thank God that he hasn't given you the spirit of fear but instead power, love, and a sound mind. Thank him that he promised in his Word to keep you in perfect peace when you concentrate on him. Then keep your focus on him instead of on all the possible outcomes. He will take care of the outcome."

"But I'm concerned what it will mean if I don't pass."

"Tell the spirit of fear the truth: God knows his plans for you—to prosper you and not to harm you, to give you a hope-filled future. God isn't pacing in heaven, wondering how you'll survive this and what he will do if you don't pass the exam. He already knows the outcome. And he promises to work *all* things together for your good and for his glory. I know this is hard, sweetheart, but you have a choice. You cannot serve two kingdoms at once. Either you trust God and his Word, or you trust the enemy of your soul who is feeding fearful thoughts into your mind. If you trust God, then you must believe he will work this out and keep you at peace while doing so.

"Find a couple Scripture passages to cling to when fearful thoughts come so that you can tell the fear to leave because you choose to believe the truth in Scripture instead. Psalm 34:4 says, 'I sought the LORD, and he answered me; he delivered me from all my fears.' Isaiah 41:10 says, 'Do not fear, for I am with you; do not anxiously look about you, for I am your God. I will strengthen you, surely I will help you' (NASB). When you recognize fear's whispers, refuse to entertain them and instead quote applicable Scripture passages to refute them.

"Instead of focusing on the problem, stay focused on the Problem Solver. We become fearful, worried, and anxious when we take our attention off God and focus on our circumstances. The key to maintaining or regaining our peace is to keep our thoughts focused on God. Isaiah 26:3 says, 'You will keep in perfect peace all who trust in you, all whose thoughts are fixed on you!' (NLT)."

I reminded him of the promise in 1 Peter 3:14: "But even if you suffer for doing what is right, God will reward you for it. So don't worry or be afraid of their threats" (NLT). We prayed, refuted the spirit of fear, and thanked God for his faithfulness in all things.

I knew the importance of the next day's exam for his future, yet I rested my head on the pillow and slept in perfect peace, knowing that God held my son's future in his hands and that he desired only the best for him. God comforted me with Proverbs 3:21–26: "My child, don't lose sight of common sense and discernment. Hang on to them, for they will refresh your soul. . . . They keep you safe on your way, and your feet will not stumble. You can go to bed without fear; you will lie down and sleep soundly. You need not be afraid of sudden disaster or the destruction that comes upon the wicked, for the LORD is your security" (NLT). God promised that for those in relationship with him, no result will ever represent defeat or disaster because the Lord will accompany, protect, and direct us. We raised our son to know God and to pursue an active relationship with him, even in times of crisis.

Ambrose Redmoon said, "Courage is not the absence of fear, but rather the judgment that something else is more important than fear."[5] My son calmed his heart and trusted God for the outcome even as he stepped through his preparation. I knew he knew the exam material.

This situation wasn't about that but about him learning to trust a faithful God and grow deeper in his relationship with him.

The next morning he texted me, "Alright! I've got the right amount of nerves, but I've got confidence in God and his willingness to help me recall!"

I knew then that he had his armor on to fight against the spirit of fear and to win, knowing truly, "But you belong to God, my dear children. You have already won a victory over those people, because the Spirit who lives in you is greater than the spirit who lives in the world" (1 John 4:4 NLT).

Laurie shared how she dealt with fear:

> Since childhood, medical procedures, shots, needles, even discussions of broken bones caused me anxiety and significant embarrassment when I passed out from fear. Dental procedures, knee surgery, tonsillectomy, and sinus surgery produced fear and anxiety but prepared me for two recent surgeries due to automobile accident injuries. The day before surgery, fears resurfaced and prompted tears.
>
> Suddenly, I realized I could cry or I could be proactive. So I spoke out loud, "Satan, you are the father of lies. God did not give us the spirit of fear but instead power, love, and a sound mind. So you can go back to hell where you came from and take this fear with you." Immediately, my fear was gone and I went about my day. Over the next twenty-four hours, that verse was my constant companion. Every time the fear tried to creep in, I spoke that verse out loud. It strengthened me. When I underwent the next surgery, I didn't experience any fear!

When Life Doesn't Go as Planned

A drive that should've taken seven or eight hours ended up taking closer to thirteen.

We stopped midway through our drive home on a holiday weekend to eat lunch at one of our favorite restaurants with friends in a city

I previously called home. Conversation flowed easily, and catching up warmed our hearts. We parted company eager to make the last leg of our drive but looking forward to seeing them again whenever God permitted.

Within moments of getting back on the interstate and getting stuck in traffic (apparently everyone else was driving home after the holiday weekend too!), my husband mentioned chest discomfort. He is *not* a complainer, so I take seriously any mention of discomfort or pain.

"It's probably just heartburn," he said, trying to allay my concerns.

In thirty years of marriage, he's never had heartburn. I messaged my three closest friends and asked them to pray for our safety and his well-being. After we finally pulled into the driveway, exhausted, he went straight to bed, still not well.

When his description changed from "discomfort" to "pain" the next morning, we immediately called the oncologist who had treated him over the last several months. She wisely advised him to go straight to the emergency room. By then, he had radiating chest pain over his shoulder and down his back, and he couldn't breathe without discomfort.

Staff immediately took blood work and obtained scans. They ran in and out of his room, checking, double-checking, and conferring before ultimately diagnosing him with multiple bilateral pulmonary embolisms due to chemotherapy thickening his blood. He disliked the prescribed treatment but acquiesced: more medication and a multiple-day hospital stay.

He looked discouraged as he relayed, "I'm sorry, honey."

Tears leaked from my eyes. "You don't need to apologize. You are where you need to be. I thank God you are here. This could have happened while we were traveling and landed you in a hospital out of state. Your doctor could have listened to you, assumed it was heartburn, and not assessed you in time. You could have thrown a clot to your heart or your brain. Don't be sorry. Be thankful. God took care of us, and we will trust him to continue."

What do we do when the diagnosis isn't what we wanted?
When the month is longer than the paycheck?
When the heartache seems too painful to bear?
When we have more questions than answers?
When people let us down?

We can become worried, anxious, and fearful, or we can trust. We can trust in a sovereign God. We can trust the One who knew the situation before it ever arose. We can trust the One who knows all the answers and provides all our help. We can believe his Word, rely on his promises, and trust his truth.

Trusting God is always our first and best option.

God is a very present help in trouble. Trusting God is always our first and best option, since he is our refuge, strength, and provider. If you struggle to trust God, you may want to review the "Five Keys to Trusting God" in chapter 2.

Our enemy screams that we should worry, fear, and even panic because he wants to steal our joy and kill our peace.

Diane said this of her struggles:

> Living with irrational fear and anxiety has been a nightmare and like a prison sentence. Fear and anxiety kept me living in a protective bubble, preventing me from experiencing life with all its blessings to its fullest with joy! With such fear and anxiety, life was just about getting through and surviving each day without incident.

God, who holds the universe in one hand and holds us close with the other, encourages us to be strong and courageous, to resist fear, to remember that he went before us to meet our needs. "Be strong and courageous. Do not be afraid or terrified because of them, for the LORD your God goes with you; he will never leave you nor forsake you" (Deut. 31:6).

My friend Karen shared her story:

I lived my whole life in fear! I was amazed because I really didn't know. When things got snug relationally or financially, I had a pit in my stomach, I shook, my breathing and heart rate increased, and it upset my digestive system. No one knew; I suffered in silence. I grew up believing I had to be perfect and wasn't supposed to talk much or have an opinion. School challenged me, but I tried hard to make good grades. Home was stressful, with lots of arguing that kept me unsettled. I walked on eggshells trying to keep peace. If placed in a sudden emergency situation, I dealt with it, then shook and second-guessed myself and feared failure.

Fear is fueled by doubt and unbelief, while the antithesis to fear is hope and faith. The by-product of faith is peace. Jesus came not only to give us peace but also to replace worry, anxiety, and fear with his peace. "Peace I leave with you; my peace I give you. I do not give to you as the world gives. Do not let your hearts be troubled and do not be afraid" (John 14:27). We must actively reject and refute the spirit of fear with God's truth, or else Jesus's gift might as well be returned "Address unknown."

Your Rx

1. Look up the following verses: Deuteronomy 31:6; Isaiah 26:3; John 14:27; and 2 Timothy 1:7. Then write them on index cards and place them where you will see them frequently. Read each of these passages aloud three times daily, committing them to memory. Ask God to give you a clearer understanding of them and to make them alive and active in your life.

2. Think back over your life. Pray and ask God to show you any times when you agreed with the spirit of fear instead of accepting God's peace. Repent of agreeing with the spirit of fear rather than with God's truths and ask God to help you trust him instead.

3. Consider times, places, situations, and circumstances when and where fear seems to lurk in your life. What triggers it? Fear is nothing more than the enemy's lie disguised as truth. What truths from God's Word can counter it? (For example, if I am prone to having a fear of lack, financially or otherwise, I can counter it with "And my God will meet all your needs according to the riches of his glory in Christ Jesus" [Phil. 4:19]).

My Prayer for You

Father, thank you for being our strength and our peace. Thank you for caring about every detail of our lives. And thank you for assuring us that you are always with us. Help the one reading these words now to feel your constant presence. Lift the full weight of worry from their shoulders. Help them cast all their cares on you, confident that you will comfort and provide for them. I ask, Father, that you will give them increased confidence in you. Help them to focus on and rest in the calmness of your loving grace despite their circumstances. Increase their ability to trust your faithfulness and your sovereign plan for their life. In Jesus's name, amen.

Recommended Playlist

"Courageous," Casting Crowns, ℗ 2011 by Provident Label Group LLC

"I Have This Hope," Tenth Avenue North, © 2016 by Provident Label Group LLC

"Good Day," Natalie Grant, ℗© 2015 by Curb Records, Inc.

"The Answer," Jeremy Camp, ℗© 2017 by Stolen Pride Records LLC

"Fear Not," Kristene DiMarco, ℗© 2017 by Bethel Music

4

Worry Creeps

And if worry can't accomplish a little thing like that, what's the use of worrying over bigger things?

Luke 12:26 NLT

Worrying does not take away tomorrow's troubles, it takes away today's peace.

Randy Armstrong

The day's to-do list would've taken longer than a week to accomplish. Yet nothing could be shaved off to make more margin. I felt crushed under its enormity. There was no way I could complete it all. Whom would I let down? My patients? My publisher? God? Me?

Then my son said, "Mom, I was thinking we could go on a date."

As an excuse formed on my lips, I could feel the room—and my emotional reserve—shrink as pictures ran through my mind like a movie.

How did I get here? (Where is that permission slip that needed signing?)

When did things get so out of control? (Did I call the insurance agent back?)

Where do I start when everything is important and something won't get done? (Do I skip a project or shopping for a friend's birthday?)

What kind of a wife am I? Mother? Employer? Friend? (Can I pick the kids up from school without running out of gas?)

My thoughts tumbled around my head like a ball in a pinball machine, setting off internal alarms and bouncing off in unexpected directions before slowly rolling past my flailing mental flippers into obscurity as the next thought rolled onto the board demanding attention and action.

Worry, doubt, and dread stand in the shadow of overwhelm. Yet those are all lies, tempting us by the father of lies, the accuser of the brethren (John 8:44; Rev. 12:10). I've taken his bait many times. Have you?

That feeling of being overwhelmed always stems from worry, which steals our peace. I frequently talk with patients and loved ones who don't realize their everyday worries add up to an uncomfortable way of living, void of the peace God promises.

Everyday worries add up to an uncomfortable way of living, void of the peace God promises.

The enemy always wins when he convinces us to divert our attention from God to the details that too frequently spur our everyday worries: to-do lists, overcrowded schedules, praiseworthy crafted holiday costumes, perfectly set dinner tables. What about the deeper issues of the heart? We focus on "impression management" with perfectly styled social media photos and status updates to engender likes, comments, and shares, as if they mean anything about our value and worth offline. We might even say yes to commitments when we'd rather not, just because we desire acceptance and affirmation. We work ourselves into a frenzy with insufficient rest because we don't trust next month's paycheck or perhaps because we've fallen victim to the lie that our worth is equal to our busyness or our possessions.

When we allow ourselves to become swallowed up in the urgency of the moment, the hour, or the day, we trade our peace for a counterfeit that never satisfies. When we aren't intentional with our thoughts and actions, our habitual way of responding to life with worry sets the stage for unrest and discontentment.

Gena put it like this:

> I used to think I was just overprotective or a worrywart. I expected the worst if someone didn't answer the phone or didn't call back in a timely manner. If my husband was late getting home from work, I imagined planning his funeral, and at times I even drove around making sure he wasn't in a ditch.

Worry opens the door for the author of confusion to write upon our hearts and minds. Jesus warned us not to worry about tomorrow. He knew temptation would come. But worrying about tomorrow only adds problems to today. "Therefore do not worry about tomorrow, for tomorrow will worry about itself. Each day has enough trouble of its own" (Matt. 6:34).

We never see Jesus worried or hurried. He had enough ministry needs to meet to last multiple lifetimes, yet he had only three years to complete the work the Father sent him to do. He wasn't ruled by to-do lists or public perception. Never once did he rush to get more done. We never read of him running to his next divine appointment. Rather, Jesus walked at a pace that was sustainable. He simply did the next thing his Father told him to do, and that was enough.

God cares greatly about us. Scripture explains that he cares about the birds and meets all their needs, yet he cares even more about us. "Look at the birds. They don't plant or harvest or store food in barns, for your heavenly Father feeds them. And aren't you far more valuable to him than they are?" (Matt. 6:26 NLT). The birds don't worry. They trust the provision of the hand that created them. We should too.

Lynne reflected on the effect worry had on her:

> For a long time, I didn't acknowledge my worry because then I'd have to face it. I didn't sleep well at night. I suffered with headaches from tension or clenching my teeth. I automatically thought the worst was going to happen when I thought of all the possible scenarios. I was paranoid about what people might think. Worry made it hard to concentrate and left me feeling indecisive and inadequate.

Worry keeps us busy doing nothing productive while stealing our joy and peace. Personally, I worry because I know my own efforts are insufficient. But we can trust that if God brings a responsibility to us, he will see us through it. Worry focuses our thoughts on our own inadequacies rather than on God's grace, mercy, and provision. Jeremiah 29:11 reminds us that God's plan for us is to prosper and not to harm us. His plans for us are always good, and his timing is always perfect.

If we walk away from the shadow of worry and choose instead to walk in the light of the cross, he extends grace, which is sufficient for that moment and the next. "Each time he said, 'My grace is all you need. My power works best in weakness.' So now I am glad to boast about my weaknesses, so that the power of Christ can work through me" (2 Cor. 12:9 NLT).

My heavenly Father makes me and my needs a priority, and I reflected this to my son that day as I accepted his offer for a date. We had a grand time, making memories and cementing his understanding of love and relationship that will far outlast the items on my to-do list. Those items got done, eventually and adequately, although honestly I don't remember what they were. Now my prayer is not that the Lord will help me get everything done but that he will show me his priorities for each day. "We can make our plans, but the LORD determines our steps" (Prov. 16:9 NLT). When we seek him first, everything else falls into place. "But seek first his kingdom and his righteousness, and all these things will be given to you as well" (Matt. 6:33).

The Worrisome Future

What about worry for the future? How often do we take our focus off the present and off God's presence and become concerned with the future, whether it be this evening, tomorrow, next week, next month, next year, or even the next decade?

My friend Patti knows this well:

> I've always been blessed with good health, strength, and no need for prescription medications in my sixties. Recently, family history and the aging process have contributed to several strange maladies. I fear growing too weak to care for our home. My husband's health has forced him to cut back, and I do more. I worry I won't be able to keep up or afford someone to do the work for us. I worry we won't be able to stay in a "real" home. I worry about life as a widow without family nearby and possible resulting depression and loneliness.

I can gallop down the mental highway faster than a kid in a candy store, grasping after every imaginable possibility and even implausibility. We've heard the statistics about how the majority of things we worry about concerning the future don't ever happen (How do they arrive at those statistics anyway? Surely if they could see inside my mind, the statistics would grow even higher!), yet we continue to let our imaginations run wild with worry, anxiety, and fear.

We catastrophize, mentally projecting ourselves to some future date, visualizing myriad tragedies befalling us or our families. The Bible says we should cast down these imaginations "and every high thing that exalteth itself against the knowledge of God, and [bring] into captivity every thought to the obedience of Christ" (2 Cor. 10:5 KJV). Scripture reveals that imaginations have consequences. "When they [the ungodly] knew God, they glorified him not as God . . . but became vain in their imaginations, and their foolish heart was darkened" (Rom. 1:21 KJV).

My friend Debbie shared her experience:

> The enemy attacks me with my vivid imagination. As a young wife and mother, I worried if my husband got home late from work or a business trip. Before cell phones, if he was more than fifteen to twenty minutes late, I worried. As time passed, the later he was, the more worry turned to fear—fear he had a car accident and was hurt, wounded, or lying dead on the side of the road. I paced the floors, thinking through every scenario in which I would find him or the police would come to my door. My mind raced, and worry overwhelmed my thoughts. The picture I visualized in my mind wasn't pretty. When he finally got home, I was so upset and angry with him because of my overwhelming worry. At that time, I didn't know how to take every thought captive, believe the best, or even trust God's care for the situation.

Worries about the future create anxiety and stress because they represent a picture that excludes God. As we project into the worrisome future, we attempt to solve the distressing situations by ourselves and for ourselves rather than trusting that God already knows, already sees, and already has solutions worked out.

Worries about the future create anxiety and stress because they represent a picture that excludes God.

The disciples worried about the future, and Jesus addressed it directly with them: "Therefore I tell you, do not worry about your life, what you will eat; or about your body, what you will wear. For life is more than food, and the body more than clothes. Consider the ravens: They do not sow or reap, they have no storeroom or barn; yet God feeds them. And how much more valuable you are than birds! Who of you by worrying can add a single hour to your life?" (Luke 12:22–25). We don't need to worry about the future or fear God's will for our lives, because he works out the very best for us. When concern about the future comes, we can recognize it and then refuse to entertain it. We can determine to stay in the present and in God's presence, trusting in his perfect plan.

Worry is the outward sign of fear, while peace is the outward sign of trust in God. Worry robs us of the peace God offers us today. We must intentionally refuse to tolerate worry. The enemy wants to keep us balled up in a worried knot, void of God's peace so that we won't move forward in the plans and destiny God has for us. But God promises something better: "But blessed is the one who trusts in the LORD, whose confidence is in him. They will be like a tree planted by the water that sends out its roots by the stream. It does not fear when heat comes; its leaves are always green. It has no worries in a year of drought" (Jer. 17:7–8).

Worry versus Trust

The summer following high school graduation, and before his departure for college, my son enrolled in flight school to obtain his private pilot's license. One day he graduated from high school, and the next he was flying while his peers vacationed, tanned, and enjoyed a carefree summer. Getting this license before starting college would allow him to skip some basics and would get him closer to being able to work as a flight instructor, helping him accrue flight hours and defray his tuition.

This was a lofty goal. Most pilots pursue private pilot certification over many months or years. He had only a couple months. We plotted out the requirements, accounted for weather cancellations, and realized that if he had any chance of accomplishing this, it would require intentionality and dedication, to the point of quitting his job and shortening our family vacation. He studied rigorously and flew almost daily throughout the summer.

He sat for the written exam and passed. In the final week before leaving for college, he needed to take a cross-country check flight, solo short and long cross-country flights, two preliminary check rides, and the big FAA practical test. That week, however, he faced one obstacle after another, from unexpected storms to an unavailability of FAA examiners to administer the practical test, none of which he controlled.

The most nerve-racking part of the situation was that he was prepared. He had done his due diligence. The flight school owner and his flight instructor, with whom he had worked daily throughout the summer, both confirmed he knew the material. In fact, he woke up in the middle of the night answering practice exam questions. He later relayed, "Mom, I was literally answering questions in my sleep."

As he studied and rehearsed answers to upcoming exam questions, I mentally rehearsed worries. Esther Hicks says, "Worrying is using your imagination to create something you don't want."[1]

He was running out of time. The university's policy stated that students had to be on campus with license in hand to earn credit and move on to the next level of training. No more days existed for makeup flights, and each section of the program required successful completion of the preceding component. If one flight didn't happen, everything had to be rescheduled. Each day clouds swelled and storms popped up out of nowhere. Several close friends prayed for him, in agreement with me, over the phone as I wrung my hands and worried about the ultimate outcome. I hated the thought of all his effort and the expense being for naught.

The last day came and went, the results not what we had hoped. We had exhausted the time for the final step. We left in the morning without license in hand, feeling crushed in spirit. He had never wanted anything so badly in his life, and honestly, I had never prayed so hard, so long, so continuously for anything for him. The license and what it represented were huge—the desire of his heart and ours. For whatever reason, it wasn't meant to be that summer.

I'll never forget as he drew me in for a hug and apologized to me, knowing the expense the situation had caused and would cause in the future. That was the least of my concerns. I cared more that he knew I was proud of him. He had given his all, and if he'd had a few more days, the result would've been different. As his mother, I couldn't have been more proud. What I didn't want him to know was that I felt let down by God. He knew my son's needs. He knew what was on the line. Surely he heard our prayers.

Sometimes when my heart is broken and my prayers are reduced to nothing but honest tears, it's best for me to get away for solitary time with God, where I rest best in his peace. That usually means sitting by a lake somewhere while the water laps at my feet and I sit still to receive whatever he needs me to hear. In the deep recesses of my soul, I knew he was still sovereign over all. Nothing takes him by surprise, and God doesn't wring his hands wondering how he will bring good from my painful circumstances.

Throughout this situation, I frequently thought back to the familiar story of Mary and Martha in Luke 10. As Jesus and the disciples traveled to Jerusalem, they stopped at Mary and Martha's home. Mary sat at Jesus's feet, listening to his teachings. But Martha was distracted by her dinner preparations. She complained to Jesus, asking him to see the unfairness of the situation and to make Mary help her in the kitchen.

Jesus replied, "My dear Martha, you are worried and upset over all these details! There is only one thing worth being concerned about. Mary has discovered it, and it will not be taken away from her" (Luke 10:41–42 NLT). The NIV says, "Mary has chosen *what is better*" (v. 42, emphasis added).

Honestly, I desire to exhibit a Mary heart, but that week in particular I could've been Martha's twin. I fretted, paced, and called in the prayer reinforcements. Sometimes as a parent, nothing will tempt us to worry more than concern for our children. Just like Martha, rather than worshiping and praising, I let the concerns that preoccupied my mind distract my heart. When the results didn't go as I'd asked or hoped for, I echoed Martha's complaint: "Lord, doesn't it seem unfair to you?"

God replied by asking, "Will you trust me? Will you trust me when you cannot see my hand at work, when you don't have all the pieces? Will you trust that I am always good and my plans for you are always good? Will you trust my heart even when you cannot see my hand? Will you choose *what is better*? Because until we settle that, nothing else matters."

Romans 15:13 says, "May the God of hope fill you with all joy and peace as you trust in him, so that you may overflow with hope by the power of the Holy Spirit." God gives us hope, joy, and peace, but we play a role. It is as we trust him that he fills us with joy and peace and we will overflow with hope.

> *Worrying never accomplishes anything, but trust opens up a world of possibility and allows God to change everything.*

I had a choice to make. I had to choose to believe truth. Worrying never accomplishes anything, but trust opens up a world of possibility and allows God to change everything. When I worry, I'm believing the enemy's lies. The enemy screamed, "God doesn't care. If he cared, you would've gotten the answer you wanted." Instead, I had to choose to believe the truth of God's Word: God is sovereign. He is for me and my son. He knows the good plans he has for me and my child, which include a hopeful future (Jer. 29:11). And he promises to work all things together for our good—even this unfortunate situation.

My tearful answer was a prayerful "Yes, Lord. I trust you. And I praise you in and through the storm. May the seeds that have been planted in faith be watered by these tears to grow a harvest for your glory."

Exchange Worry for Bold Courage

Do you ever slip in your struggles and become ill-footed with worry rather than stand on the solid ground of God's promises? Do others evoke fear and trembling by barking orders and demands or threatening to throw you to the hungry lions waiting to devour their prey? If so, you're in good company! But you're also in the perfect position for protection and provision, which will be for your good and for your Father's glory.

Daniel found himself there. The king had elevated him over jealous rivals who set out to trap him by convincing the king to outlaw worship of anyone but the king. Daniel had a choice to make. He could deny his devotion to God and fearfully acquiesce to the new law. He could remain devoted to God and worry about the consequences from the king. Or he could remain steadfast in his faith and trust God in the midst of the situation. Daniel continued to pray thrice daily, kneeling in front of a window in view of his detractors.

His jealous peers saw him and snitched to the king, who was forced to punish him according to the decree, putting him in the lions' den. The king, who hadn't wanted to punish Daniel, ran to the lions' den the morning after Daniel was incarcerated and found him unharmed. "The king was overjoyed and ordered that Daniel be lifted from the den. Not a scratch was found on him, *for he had trusted in his God*" (Dan. 6:23 NLT, emphasis added).

This represents a great lesson for us. Worldly pressures can cause us to cave and compromise, or worry about the consequences, or both. Yet Daniel faced his situation with integrity and refused to compromise. He trusted God and refused to worry. *Then* God met Daniel's needs and rewarded his trust by keeping him safe in a den full of lions. Since God protected Daniel, don't you think he will be faithful to his promises and provide for us also? God repeatedly tells us in his Word to be of bold courage and not to worry or fear.

Your Rx

1. Look up the following verses: Matthew 6:34; Luke 10:42; and Romans 15:13. Then write them on index cards and place them where you will see them frequently. Read each of these passages aloud three times daily, committing them to memory.

2. Think about what situations cause you to worry the most. What would you gain by choosing to trust God instead?

Ask him to help you replace worry with trust in him and his provision.

3. Reflect on and then record three incidents from your past when you worried but now can see that God was faithful and provided for your needs.

My Prayer for You

Father, you know the days are long and the pressures are many. I thank you that while we may plan our course, you establish our steps. I thank you that you know the plans you have for us and that they are plans to prosper us and not to harm us, plans for a future and a hope. I pray now, Lord, that you will help us to lay down our worries and instead trust in your perfect provision. Help us to recognize that when we worry, we believe the enemy's convincing lies rather than trust in your promises. Thank you that you promise to meet our every need and that you care for us even more than you care for the flowers in the field and the birds in the air. We love you and trust you. In Jesus's name, amen.

Recommended Playlist

"Oh My Soul," Casting Crowns, ℗ 2016 by Provident Label Group LLC

"Right on Time," Aaron Cole and Toby Mac, ℗© 2017 by Gotee Records

"Find You Here," Ellie Holcomb, © 2017 by Full Heart Music

"God I Look to You," Bethel Music, ℗© 2014 by Bethel Music

"Near to Me," I AM THEY, © 2018 by Provident Label Group LLC

5

Anxiety Seeps

Whatever you have learned or received or heard from me, or seen in me—put it into practice. And the God of peace will be with you.

Philippians 4:9

Our anxiety does not come from thinking about the future, but from wanting to control it.

Kahlil Gibran

"I hate to tell you this, but you need to get your affairs in order."

How could that be? My husband wasn't yet forty. After several years of a commuter marriage, we again lived under the same roof. We had new jobs and a toddler. Until this moment, we felt like the sun was rising for us.

Fear and worry immediately assaulted me, and anxiety seeped into my core.

I experienced fatherlessness as a teenager: mine died from a fatal heart attack when he was forty-two. I remembered the pain from the lack, and now I imagined the same for my son. Fortunately, as a toddler, he was too young to feel cancer's sharp tear at the fabric of our family's tapestry.

While doctors predicted my husband would live only a couple years, God had a different plan. He is, after all, the One who plans our days and orders our steps.

Still, even after treatment concluded, we continued to return every three months, then every six, then eventually yearly for repeat imaging and blood draws to monitor for a relapse. Each visit we held our breath, wondering, *What if?*

What if the treatment didn't work?

What if the cancer returns?

What if he doesn't defy the odds?

What if the scan doesn't show what's really there?

What if the cancer metastasizes as predicted?

What if . . . ?

That's the nature of anxiety. Anxiety often starts from something small: "What if she doesn't return my call?" "What if I don't lose this weight?" "What if they don't like my outfit?" Then if not addressed, anxiety seeps into our lives and spreads like water from a leaky roof to damage everything it touches. "What if I die miserable, friendless, and alone?" "What if I become obese and die from a heart attack or lose my limbs to diabetes?" "What if everyone in the room laughs at me and it's posted on YouTube?"

Anxiety results from living in a place of defeat instead of victory. When we are anxious, we assume problems will occur rather than having faith that God has already gone before us to work everything out for our good and for his glory. God's way is best: "I will go before you and will level the mountains. . . . I will give you hidden treasures, riches stored in secret places, so that you may know that I am the LORD, the God of Israel, who summons you by name" (Isa. 45:2–3). "Do not be afraid or discouraged, for the LORD will personally go ahead of you. He will be with you; he will neither fail you nor abandon you" (Deut. 31:8 NLT).

We must face the consequences of living and coping our own way. After years of my questioning, pleading, and prayerfully relinquishing my doubts, fears, and concerns at the cross, God turned the tables and asked me the most important question.

"What if . . . you trusted me? What if you believed that the same God who defied the odds before and healed your husband of cancer the first time can protect him and you in all your tomorrows?"

Anxiety results from living in a place of defeat instead of victory.

Wow. Yes, Lord. What if?

He was teaching me the power of two little words: What if?

The enemy of our souls uses those two words against us to incite anxiety. Those two words steal our peace from today as we anxiously focus on tomorrow rather than sitting in God's presence and resting in the present.

Everyone has anxious thoughts at times because we are limited creatures. We don't know what tomorrow will bring. None of us has the ability to control the world we live in, yet we desire to.

Diana described her experience:

> My marriage was troubled, my youngest son struggled in school, I couldn't work because of migraines, and finances were tight. The fear of failure weighed me down. Consumed with anxiety, I dwelled on the what-ifs of life.

Jodi shared her challenges:

> As a newlywed, I suffered significant anxiety. My military husband deployed for months at a time. I became increasingly agitated. Racing thoughts robbed me of sleep. I lay awake at night, elaborately planning how to respond to an intruder. I stayed up increasingly later, avoiding bedtime. Despite our limited income, I begged for a home alarm system for assurance it never offered. After my son was born, my fears of What if? intensified: What if my house burns down?

> What if we are robbed? What if something happens to my baby?

Jesus offers the antidote. Jesus said, "Don't let your hearts be troubled. Trust in God, and trust also in me" (John 14:1 NLT). It's a matter of the will. He said, "Don't *let* your hearts be troubled." It's a choice. We must choose not to become anxious and troubled. Instead, we must trust in God.

Fast-forward fifteen years. My husband and I experienced an all-too-similar scenario. The day we had looked forward to for years, the day of my first book's release, we heard the words we had prayed we'd never hear again: "Your biopsy results came back positive. You have cancer."

The doctor explained that my husband did not have a recurrence of the original disease. The current cancer was considered a secondary cancer, probably resulting from the original chemotherapy treatment.

Immediately, our focus shifted from release party festivities, interviews, book signings, and marketing plans to blood work, PET scans, bone marrow biopsies, port placements, and more doctor visits than we could remember without a calendar. Sadly, my mind ran back to, What if?

What if the very thing that was used to save his life before is what kills him now?

What if we aren't so "lucky" and the chemotherapy doesn't work this time?

What if the chemotherapy for the current cancer results in another future cancer diagnosis?

What if my sons have to grow up without their dad?

What if I become a widow?

What if . . . ?

I jumped into an old, familiar coping pattern: staying busy. I alerted family and friends of the news and answered the plethora of questions with what little sure information we had. I prepared freezer meals for the weeks when doctors' appointments and chemotherapy treatments would keep us too busy to shop or cook. I rearranged my work schedule to accommodate the myriad new appointments that took priority.

In my effort to control the uncontrollable, the busyness overwhelmed me and left me depleted and exhausted until finally one day I collapsed in a pile on the floor and wept. How had I gotten here, and what was I going to do?

As I desperately cried out to God, I heard his familiar question yet again: "What if . . . you trusted me?"

> What if you believed that this didn't take me by surprise? (Ps. 139:16; Matt. 6:8).
>
> What if you believed I really do work all things together for your good? (Rom. 8:28).
>
> What if you remembered I know the plans I have for you, and I have declared that my plans for you are good, and they include a future and a hope? (Jer. 29:11).
>
> What if you remembered I am good, my ways are good, and my love for you is everlasting? (Jer. 31:3).
>
> What if you remembered I proved myself faithful to you when you went through this before, and knowing I am the same yesterday, today, and tomorrow, you believed I will be faithful through this as well? (Heb. 13:8).
>
> What if you stopped listening to the father of lies, who fills your mind with what-ifs, kept your eyes on me, and listened only to the voice of your heavenly Father, who speaks truth and love? (John 17:17).

As I dried my tears and finished my prayer time with the Lord, I found a new determination to let go of the anxiety-producing what-ifs and take hold of the prevailing peace God promises. Because even *if,*

God is still big enough to handle whatever comes my way, and none of it takes him by surprise.

The Desire for Control

So often anxiety seeps into our lives through an otherwise generally minor event (e.g., the vacuum cleaner breaks before company arrives to spend the weekend, emergency car repairs temporarily tap the savings account, or turbulence on an airplane takes place) as the enemy of our souls whispers to our hearts and minds, "What if?"

What if my guest thinks I'm a bad housekeeper?

What if our savings is depleted?

What if the plane crashes?

Shonda disclosed:

> I worried about how we'd recover from a financial crisis of our own doing. We had launched our own business but had to charge furnishings, marketing, and publicity expenses. We stepped out in faith. Yet I feared and questioned, "What if the business doesn't succeed or pay back our debts? Those fears came to pass, and we had no way to pay our debts, forcing us to file for Chapter 13 bankruptcy. I imagined our future: How much will we lose in the bankruptcy? How will we fare financially? What will people think of me? Will the church reject us? Is God mad? What will this do to our reputation? I isolated myself, cried, and had fits. In fearful anger, I fussed at and blamed my family. I ate excessively and slept throughout the day to avoid facing anyone and my own thoughts. I couldn't turn off my brain unless I slept.

When we don't address anxiety appropriately, it expands to fill the territory we give it (including all our thoughts). Our minds amplify the daily annoyance or frustration of "What if I can't vacuum before company comes?" to a more concerning "What if they think

I am a bad housekeeper?" to the catastrophic "I'll never have any friends."

We so easily agree with the lies from the spirit of fear regarding every aspect of our lives. We become anxious and fret over our children's well-being, finances, relationships, health concerns, the future, really anything that we value and that threatens to remove our fantasy of being in control.

Kelly described her experience:

> I experienced tightness in my chest. It was as if life was trying to strangle peace out of me. This occurred when I felt out of control. Usually, it was something I feared, couldn't handle, or couldn't manage. My body responded when my words couldn't. Then I'd feel ashamed about my anxiety. This made me worry I would never be better or do better. It was a cycle of continual nervousness I couldn't escape from.

Ever since the serpent entered the Garden of Eden, we have fought to gain and maintain control of every aspect of our lives. Adam and Eve had the God of all creation as their walking companion and provider, yet they desired control rather than allowing God to continue to supply their every need.

How often do we worry about all the details . . . only to have everything work out fine and to discover we sacrificed our peace for nothing?

We've all experienced it. We wake up and before our feet even hit the ground, anxiety over the day ahead starts to build as we mentally review the day's tasks: shower and dress, take the kids to school, make the overdue dentist appointment, don't forget the dry cleaning for the second day in a row, order the birthday cake . . . Before we've made it through the first task on the ever-present to-do list, we feel overwhelmed by the thought of it all. Ultimately, we feel overwhelmed because we feel we are not in control of our circumstances.

Remember our discussion of Martha in chapter 4? That's exactly what happened to her. She opened her home to Jesus and his disciples. "Martha was distracted by all the preparations that had to be made" (Luke 10:40), while her sister, Mary, listened at Jesus's feet. Frustrated and angry that Mary didn't help prepare, Martha fumed to Jesus, asking him to make Mary help. Martha possessed good motives— Scripture says the preparations *had to be made*—but her heart was in an overwhelmed tizzy. Martha felt overwhelmed by all that had to be done, and she was unable to control the situation or others in it, so she essentially asked Jesus to help her regain control by making Mary help her. Jesus calmly redirected her attention to the heart of the matter: Martha was anxious and worried about many things instead of appreciating his presence.

Jesus essentially conveyed that if she would relinquish the need for control and focus her attention on him instead of the details, everything would fall into place and peace. How often do we worry about all the details, the what-ifs and the what-could-bes, only to have everything work out fine and to discover we sacrificed our peace for nothing?

> *Faith entails having the courage to give God control.*

James 4:7 says, "Submit yourselves, then, to God. Resist the devil, and he will flee from you." If we do not submit to God, we leave an opening for the enemy's influence. The key is to first submit ourselves to God, recognizing that his will and his way protect and provide. *Then* knowing we are securely held in his care, we can resist the enemy's temptation to worry and watch him flee. We are not responsible for the things that tempt us to become anxious, but we have to be willing to let go of them.

God desires to meet our needs, yet he will not fight us for control. In sailing, two captains cannot both steer the ship. The same is true in our lives. We can give the enemy control, attempt to take control, or surrender and allow God to be in control. Faith entails having the courage to give God control.

A Little Word Makes *All* the Difference

Do you ever sense God trying to get your attention, trying to tell you something, but you don't want to hear it? I recently sensed God saying, "You say you trust me, but do you trust me in *all* things?"

God had me camp in Romans 8:28: "And we know that in *all* things God works for the good of those who love him, who have been called according to his purpose" (emphasis added).

The word *all* leapt off the page. If I really trust God, then do I trust that he will bring good from a disappointing day? From a difference of opinion with a loved one? From a chronic illness? From a business transaction that didn't go as expected? From the death of a friend?

If I trust that his Word is true, then I must trust that everything he says is true. Not just for others but also for me. Not just the parts I like but the uncomfortable parts too.

I felt overwhelmed by the lengthy to-do list and the short time span in which to accomplish it. I didn't even know where to start. I felt weary, a sure sign I carried things not meant for me to carry. In my heart, I heard his plea: "Give *all* your anxiety to me because I care for you" (see 1 Pet. 5:7).

I knew he cared about my patient with progressing dementia, but did he also care about my ongoing pain? Or the house that needed cleaning and the meal I needed to plan and make before company arrived? What about the bills that needed paying? My lonely son at camp?

He said to give him *all* my anxiety. Not just some, not just what I feel comfortable with or desperate to give, but all. Why? Because he cares for me. Because he cares for me, I can trust him.

We can trust him in *all* things. God never tells us to do something without also giving us the solution for the problem. When God gives us a command such as "Be anxious for nothing," he also gives us the means to obey. It comes by trusting him.

Either Jesus walked on water or he didn't. Either God heals or he doesn't. Either Jesus rose from the dead or he didn't. We either believe him and the Word or we don't. It's *all* or nothing. For me, that three-letter word *all* makes all the difference.

Taking Things into Our Own Hands

The things God calls me to trust him with are relatively small compared to those of Abraham. Abraham and Sarah didn't have children. We know that Abraham and Sarah struggled with letting God be in control of their situation because in Genesis, Sarah took the situation into her own hands. In fact, she blamed God. "The LORD has kept me from having children" (Gen. 16:2). Then she told Abraham to go sleep with her slave Hagar to build a family through her. Clearly, Sarah struggled to trust that God would faithfully fulfill his promise to give them children. But when Abraham was one hundred, Isaac was born in fulfillment of God's promise to Abraham and Sarah twenty-five years earlier.

Can you imagine, then, what Abraham must have felt, after having waited an entire century to be a father, when God asked him to take his son up a mountain and sacrifice (kill) him as a burnt offering? Yet Genesis 22 reveals that Abraham did not appear to have hesitated. And what I find notable, second only to Abraham's immediate obedience to God's request, is his faith-filled response to Isaac's question.

"Isaac spoke up and said to his father Abraham, 'Father?' 'Yes, my son?' Abraham replied. 'The fire and wood are here,' Isaac said, 'but where is the lamb for the burnt offering?' Abraham answered, 'God himself will provide the lamb for the burnt offering, my son'" (Gen. 22:7–8).

Can you imagine being Isaac, accepting your father's answer while he ties twine around you and places you on an altar? What an amazing example of trusting God in everything, believing he will supply *all* your needs! If God did that for Isaac and Abraham, we can rely on God to care for us today. Faith isn't a feeling but rather trusting

God when the future appears uncertain. Instead of anxiety, faith and trust in an unfailing God should be our default.

Your Rx

1. Look up the following verses: John 14:1; Romans 8:28; and 1 Peter 5:7. Then write them on index cards and place them where you will see them frequently. Read each of these passages aloud three times daily, committing them to memory.
2. What things are you trying to maintain control of that God is asking you to surrender to him? Write them on a piece of paper. Now rip the paper up as an offering to God and an act of surrender. Prayerfully give them to God and throw away the pieces.
3. God wants us to trust him in *all* things. In what areas are you struggling to trust him? Will you pray about them, thankfully share your concerns with God, and then trust him with the outcome? He wants you to have his peace.

My Prayer for You

Father, you know that when the enemy is given even a crack, he pushes the door open wide and brings with him thoughts that produce worry, anxiety, and fear. But we can be thankful that no circumstance that confronts us ever takes you by surprise. We thank you that you promise to work all things together for our good. We thank you that you are good, your ways are good, and your love for us is everlasting. Thank you, Father, for repeatedly proving yourself faithful and that we can rest in the knowledge that you will supply all our needs in your perfect timing according to your perfect plan for our lives. We choose to trust you rather than become anxious, because you, God, are in control. In Jesus's name, amen.

Recommended Playlist

"Holding My World," Kristian Stanfill, ℗ 2011 by sixsteps-records / Sparrow Records

"Whole Heart," Brandon Heath, ℗ 2017 by Provident Label Group LLC

"No Longer Afraid," Anastasia Fomenko, ℗© 2018 by Anastasia Fomenko

"Peace Be Still," Lauren Daigle, ℗© 2017 by TBCO Music

"No Longer Slaves," Bethel Music, ℗© 2015 by Bethel Music

6

Crises Explode

I have told you these things, so that in me you may have peace. In this world you will have trouble. But take heart! I have overcome the world.

John 16:33

It is worms which destroy a tree,
it is worry which destroys a man.

Turkish proverb

At some point, we will all experience crises. Those times feel like a one-two-three punch that leaves us reeling, struggling to stand. Crises are ready fodder for worry, anxiety, and fear.

Peg shared her experience:

> Heat exhaustion, a cheating husband, financial issues— the perfect storm for anxiety and panic attacks. Doing something as simple as going to the grocery store became difficult. If I made it to the store, I feared I wouldn't make it through the checkout without experiencing those

> terrifying moments that occurred suddenly: weakness,
> light-headedness, the feeling of dread, wondering if I'd pass
> out and make a spectacle of myself. I feared losing control.
> I distracted myself so I didn't focus on those feelings as I
> waited to check out. I read the *Enquirer* headlines . . . counted
> the change in my purse . . . prayed. I felt flushed. My insides
> shook. But I didn't pass out. I didn't lose control. Victory! A
> small one, but a victory nonetheless. Every battle won was a
> step forward in defeating the anxiety.

Many people don't consider themselves worriers or anxious individuals, but when a crisis hits, they succumb. They can't think clearly. They begin doing, planning, and even course correcting, and their minds automatically jump to a fear-filled future.

In the absence of truth, our minds go to the darkest place. Our thoughts hastily ride the elevator from the penthouse to the basement. We rapidly translate "Your blood markers are abnormal" into "I'm going to die." That instantaneous mental plummet is in direct opposition to Jesus's command: "Don't *let* your hearts be troubled. Trust in God, and trust also in me" (John 14:1 NLT, emphasis added).

Jesus made this statement as if it is a choice: "Don't *let* your hearts be troubled." Decide that you won't get upset when not only did you get passed over for the promotion but you've been let go altogether. Choose not to be troubled when your spouse engages in adultery and serves you with divorce papers. Intentionally determine not to worry when the doctor calls to say the mammogram wasn't clean and you have breast cancer. Is it really that easy?

When I was a young mother, with a toddler at home and a new career recently launched, my husband received the shattering diagnosis of a very rare form of abdominal cancer. Doctors offered a two-year prognosis. Don't *let* your hearts be troubled? I didn't do a good job choosing to trust rather than to worry! I mentally envisioned myself as a widow and a single mother—lonely, sad, and abandoned.

My mother was left a young widow and a single mother to two young children, so when my husband's cancer diagnosis rocked our lives, the enemy used it as a playground for worry, anxiety, and fear, and I *let* my heart grow troubled.

First, my husband underwent an extensive, almost twenty-four-hour surgery, with a one-in-four chance of dying. Afterward, he endured months of chemotherapy and the typical side effects, including nausea, infections, dehydration, and blockages requiring numerous hospitalizations and procedures. During that year, I rarely prayed for strength or endurance to survive the day but frequently asked God for help to endure the next five minutes because I couldn't without his help.

A decade later, my husband's survival amazed doctors. It was nothing short of God's miraculous intervention, for which we were grateful beyond imagination. So, stunned is an understatement when on the day my book *Hope Prevails* released, fifteen years after his original diagnosis, the same surgeon gave him a new cancer diagnosis. Neither of us expected that.

> *True peace is not the absence of trouble but resting in the sovereignty of God in the midst of it.*

Don't *let* your heart be troubled? It was a choice. A matter of intention. A matter of recognizing God's faithfulness in the past and his promise to remain faithful in the future, even when life doesn't go as we expected or desired. It required telling the tempting worries, "No!" and enlisting faith to instead say, "God, I choose to trust you in this." True peace is not the absence of trouble but resting in the sovereignty of God in the midst of it.

Take a Deep Breath

We walked into the hospital hand in hand, neither of us speaking. Words weren't necessary. We knew the other's thoughts, what we wondered and hoped. As we sat in the oncology waiting room, I felt my tight shoulders rise near my ears. They carried the weight of our fears. They held the concerns never voiced.

I looked at him as he tried to busy himself updating paperwork. He held his breath. I did too. We always walk into these visits holding our breath, figuratively and often literally. We're never sure what the test results will reveal, what the doctor will report. So unconsciously, we held our breath while we held each other's hand, and together we held on to God to get us through.

I was blessed that my husband displayed a great attitude. This was not our first cancer rodeo. We knew that God healed him from his first and second bouts of cancer. I'm convinced, however, that his positive attitude and steadfast faith played a crucial role. Our faith is firmly planted in God. Even now, we continue to believe that God will heal him of this cancer.

Even with our strong faith, we needed to remind each other to *breathe*!

I reminded myself that God wasn't wondering how he would handle the results or how he would respond if bad test results came back or the doctor delivered an unfavorable report. God already knew the answers we needed. He already knew the outcome. He knew how he'd handle it, and he knew how he'd get us through the difficult times (Isa. 52:12).

Whatever you face today, let me offer you this hope-filled perspective: God already has it figured out. He sees you, he knows the storm you battle, and he knows how he will get you from this side to the other.

When faced with a crisis, take a deep breath. Then look to him. Keep your focus on him, not on the storms, the worries, or the fears. Be boldly courageous and keep your eyes on the Father, because he has all the answers. Thank him through the situation. Praise him through it. The enemy will attempt to distract you with worry, anxiety, and fear, but there is a reason God said, "Be anxious for nothing." Be anxious for *no thing*! If we refuse to entertain anxiety and instead pray about everything, remain thankful, and share our needs with God, *then* our hearts and minds will remain at peace (Phil. 4:6–7).

Cement Your Beliefs

As I sat in the cold, sterile recovery room waiting for my husband to wake up from anesthesia, I reflected on "real life" for us and many who shared their stories with me. From mountain highs to valley lows . . . these were all messages I received:

"Here's the latest picture of our newest grandbaby!"

"Please pray for my son. He's in trouble with the law."

"I'm sending a 'save the date' for our daughter's wedding."

"I need your prayers. Divorce appears the only option."

With my husband's new cancer diagnosis, our attention switched from celebrating my book's release to scheduling procedures and starting treatments. Over the course of weeks, days, and even moments, we, too, bounced from mountain highs to valley lows, because of either our own circumstances or the circumstances of those we loved. In my quiet time, God reminded me of the familiar story of Peter and his famous water-walking escapade in Matthew 14.

When the disciples saw Jesus walking on the lake, they were terrified, thinking he was a ghost. But Jesus revealed himself and told them to take courage and not fear. Essentially, he told them they had a choice to make: to choose courage over fear. Peter did so when he set himself apart from the others by saying, "Lord, if it's you, . . . tell me to come to you on the water" (Matt. 14:28). Jesus beckoned him to come. So Peter stepped out of the boat and onto the water and began walking toward Jesus. When he took his eyes off Jesus and looked at the wind, he became afraid, began to sink, and asked Jesus to save him. Jesus immediately caught Peter and asked him why he doubted.

Typically, when discussing this passage, people emphasize Peter's faith crisis. Yet of all the disciples, Peter was the one who recognized Jesus, demonstrated his faith, left the boat, and walked toward him. The others waited until Jesus calmed the storm before declaring him the Son of God.

Peter knew his Savior and exercised his faith by leaving the boat despite the storm surrounding him. As long as he looked at the Savior, he remained on his feet. Humanly speaking, the water wasn't safe. It wasn't dry ground, and walking on it wasn't a rational decision. But as long as he kept his eyes on Jesus, trusting him, walking on water was doable and the right thing. All of faith is about stepping into something that doesn't seem possible, trusting God in the unknown. Peter's faith crisis occurred only when he took his eyes off Jesus and paid more attention to the winds than to the One who could calm the wind in a single breath. When he focused on his circumstances, the storm, and the impossibility of his situation, the waves pulled him down.

Jesus's rebuke of Peter's doubt highlights the importance of knowing what we believe before we leave the boat, before a crisis hits. Jesus basically told Peter, "If you had determined to trust me no matter what and kept your eyes on me, you never would have faltered." How often is that true of us? If we fully trusted God in our relationships, finances, health, and other areas, then worry, anxiety, and fear wouldn't breed doubt. Instead, we would remain in his peace. Our focus must remain on him, not on our situation.

I can relate to Peter. Can you? I profess my faith in God and his power to save. But when the crises and storms of life whip around me, I often falter, focusing on the storm rather than on him, forgetting what I believe. Instead, I need to remember Psalm 121:1–2: "I lift up my eyes to the hills. From where does my help come? My help comes from the LORD, who made heaven and earth" (ESV). We must believe God's truth and keep our eyes on him, not the storms that threaten to pull us under.

I believe:

- God has always been faithful, and he will remain faithful.
- With God's help, I can make it through every difficult life circumstance.
- God warned that storms and trials would come, but *he* overcame them all. That's where our faith must rest.

- Sometimes God doesn't calm the storm, but he meets us in its midst and shows us that he can be trusted to carry us through.
- Whether we are on mountain highs or valley lows, God is the One who stills the storms.

I also realized that our crises don't take Jesus by surprise. He's already there . . . God's presence comforts us in all our storms. He is close to the brokenhearted and rescues those crushed in spirit (Ps. 34:18).

I am thankful for the times when I began to sink because they reminded me to refocus my gaze on God. He often calls us out to places that don't make sense, that without him would leave us drowning, and that require our wholehearted trust in him. Just as Peter cried out, "Lord, save me," we, too, are encouraged to cry out to him in our need and find his steady hand reaching out for us. In crises, we can focus on him, not on our storms. We can trust what we know to be true despite what we see. We are never guaranteed tomorrow, but we are guaranteed that with each tomorrow, as we walk into the unknown, he will go with us, guide us, and protect us. Our job is to trust him. I don't know your current season, but we all have a choice to make: to either focus on our storms or on the One who can calm every storm.

We are never guaranteed tomorrow, but we are guaranteed that with each tomorrow, as we walk into the unknown, he will go with us, guide us, and protect us. Our job is to trust him.

Stand on Truth

"I must be dreaming. This is too surreal to be true." I looked for any sign that life had not just changed faster than I could blink back the tears. What began as a normal day quickly plummeted, leaving me breathless and searching for answers to unthinkable questions. I prayerfully pleaded, "God, where are you? Don't you care? You could have prevented this or at least protected me from it."

We continued to battle through my husband's cancer treatment when yet another tsunami of instability rocked our lives. Multiple friends received diagnoses, we needed to make major house repairs, and we faced staffing instability at my private practice. I couldn't fathom how we'd get through these newest trials or why God had allowed them when we still wrestled with life-or-death issues.

One moment I possessed the utmost confidence we'd survive these challenges unscathed, just as we had survived every other trial we'd ever encountered—with God's help. The next moment I wavered and feared all the uncertainties and an unknown future, afraid of everything I couldn't see or control.

I also experienced intermittent anger because God hadn't done what I thought he could or should have done. "Really, God? Couldn't you have given us a brief respite to catch our breath before the next wave dragged us under?" I felt like a human version of a Magic 8 Ball, with my emotions and responses as capricious as the next shake.

My usually optimistic husband walked in at day's end and exclaimed, "Today stunk! *But* it will be redeemed!" He offered what I needed then: hope. Normally, people considered me the Hope Girl or Dr. Hope. But I didn't feel like either at that moment. Grief briefly overwhelmed me, and I needed to borrow his hope. I knew hope prevails, but I needed to appropriate his hope while God strengthened mine.

As word of our crises spread, some inquired, "What are you going to do?" We don't plan or control crises, but rather, we react to them. Proverbs 16:9 declares, "We can make our plans, but the LORD determines our steps" (NLT).

My husband and I determined to:

- pray for wisdom and direction
- not react in fear but instead follow God's lead
- stand on truth rather than rely on our feelings

We stood on these truths:

- God is with us and knows what is going to happen and the solution he will provide (Phil. 4:19).
- God is for us, not against us (Rom. 8:31).
- God cares for us, he loves us with an everlasting love, and his mercies are new every morning (Lam. 3:22–23).
- God has always been and will remain faithful (1 Cor. 1:9).
- God knows his good plans for us, which will not harm us (Jer. 29:11).
- What the enemy intended for harm, God will use for our good (Gen. 50:20).
- No storm is too big when we have faith in God (Isa. 43:2–3).

We chose to trust God's promise, "My God will meet all your needs" (Phil. 4:19). Do you see what I see? God will meet *all* our needs. Not some, not a few . . . *all*. I don't know how or when, but I trust his perfect way and perfect time. When tempted to worry or fear, let's stand on the truth that God is bigger than what we see, what we feel, what we hear on the news. He created the universe; he stills storms, heals cancer, restores relationships, and regenerates finances. Thank him now *in faith* for what he is already doing.

When crisis hits, we can face the facts while remembering his truth. We don't have to accept the facts as the final say. We can remember, "We are afflicted in every way, but not crushed; perplexed, but not despairing; persecuted, but not forsaken; struck down, but not destroyed" (2 Cor. 4:8–9 NASB). Truth, not facts, gets the last word.

My husband and I possessed no answers but trusted the One who did. We believed his Word and stood on the truth. Doing so offered peace in the midst of the storm.

Resist the Enemy's Lies

Crises overwhelm our maximum capabilities, test our limits, and threaten our resolve. They are never convenient, nor do they allow for planning or forewarning. Determining in advance our coping strategies, what mind-set we will possess, and the attitude we will maintain helps us endure when crises hit.

While moving our eldest son into his Florida coast college dorm, we scrambled to help him complete additional requirements for his freshman year that had previously been unclear. As parents, we helped navigate the challenges while also raising bunk beds, installing electronics, attending orientation sessions, and keeping one eye and ear on reports of Hurricane Harvey moving toward our Texas coast. Family and friends warned of the expected path of the storm, hotel closures along our fifteen-hundred-mile route home, and shortages of food, water, and gasoline in our area.

After arriving safely home, we watched with the rest of the nation as Hurricane Harvey stalled over Texas, causing extreme damage to the fourth largest city in our country and surrounding areas. Meanwhile, we continued to navigate early college challenges from afar. Approximately a week later, forecasters raised concern that Hurricane Irma, rising in the Atlantic, was headed for the United States and was predicted to be our country's biggest and costliest storm.

We stayed in contact with our son, trying to proactively determine the safest course of action should Irma turn toward his location. He didn't have a vehicle, so while several friends offered to host him, reaching them proved a challenge. Others were in coastal or flood areas that offered no safety. We felt powerless to keep our child safe and depended on him and news reports to help us make appropriate plans and our best decisions. My husband and I had survived Hurricane Andrew in Florida almost three decades earlier, and the images of those still without provisions following Harvey remained fresh in our minds.

Approximately ten days after we had left him at college, our son texted us shortly after midnight to inform us that another local university had ordered a mandatory evacuation. A similar order came from his university shortly thereafter. Within a span of forty-eight hours, our lives spun into crisis.

- I struggled with a weeklong unremitting barometric-change-induced migraine compliments of Harvey.
- I endured one of my most challenging weeks with patients in my private practice.
- One of our best employees resigned because of relocation.
- My husband visited his oncologist.
- My soon-to-be-released *Hope Prevails Bible Study*[1] had a publishing glitch that needed remedying.
- And most importantly, our new coastal college student needed to evacuate without a vehicle or a known place to go.

My life felt suspended as chaos swirled around me and the United States waited, watched, and prepared for the impending storm to strike. My heart lodged in my throat. My shoulders sank. I couldn't concentrate. I flitted between tasks, finishing nothing. Even my conversations were unfocused. All symptoms of anxiety.

While we strategized to determine the best way to keep our son safe despite the unpredictability of the impending storm, I simultaneously felt compelled to watch the news and weather and yet couldn't bear to. I grieved over the images of decimated Barbuda and ravaged Puerto Rico. My heart ached thinking not only of my son but also of my other loved ones in Florida who might soon be in a similar situation. Potentially being out of contact with my son choked me up every time I considered it. I navigated the release of the Bible study and determined how to handle patient demand while half staffed at my office. Time didn't afford the luxury of curling up in a ball and pulling blankets over my head.

We heard reports of stores north of my son's university that were depleted of food, water, and gas. What if he evacuated but couldn't find enough gas to exit the state safely?

The news, confirmed by family reports, showed images of seventeen lanes of traffic, including all shoulders of the highways, trying to escape Florida simultaneously, moving five miles per hour. What if people got stranded on those highways in the middle of nature's fury?

I can't tell you what prompted the change, but I finally realized that the anxiety and fear that ruled my life didn't serve me well and were counterproductive. Instead of fear, anger ensued—anger at the enemy who enticed me to believe his lies.

"Your son might not make it out of Florida safely."

"Your family may die in this storm."

"You won't find a replacement for your staff."

Our pastor announced, "You are the most resilient family I've ever met!" Honestly, credit wasn't due us, but to God who repeatedly proved his faithfulness to us, like he had with his disciples. We, like them, must trust him.

I consciously decided to rule my thoughts rather than allow them to rule me. I knew God hadn't given me the fear; it had come from my enemy. I repented for agreeing with the spirit of fear. Then I rebuked the spirit in Jesus's name and trusted God for his power, love, and sound mind.

Friend, I don't know what you currently face—natural disaster aftermath; health, relationship, or financial crisis; or something else.

I lived there—fighting many battles concurrently. Every day, but especially during crises, we must remember that as God's children we have authority and victory over the spirit of fear because God in us is greater than our enemy (1 John 4:4).

The enemy deafens us with his screams. But I refused to cave in to his bullying, his threats, and his lies. God still inhabits his throne! God still calms storms! God still heals! God still provides! Jesus said we would do greater works than Jesus did in his name (John 14:12–13). As God reminded me of this truth, I spoke to the storm and commanded it to be still in Jesus's name, both the physical hurricane and the rumbling in my heart.

At the same time, I thanked God in advance that he still rules the oceans and subdues storms (Ps. 89:9) and that he could still the waves and calm the storm to a whisper (Ps. 107:29). I thanked him for the surety that he faithfully answers our prayers with awesome deeds (Ps. 65:5).

Where does our faith reside? We must pray, believing God, not our challenges. Hank Paulson, Treasury secretary at the outset of the financial crisis of 2008 said, "During the days, I was too busy to be fearful, but I had to deal with raw fear when I woke up at night and big problems seemed insurmountable. I had a number of terror-filled nights when I looked into the abyss and saw food lines and Great Depression-like scenarios . . . we relied very heavily on prayer. Prayer is a big part of my life and looking to a higher power, a divine mind as a source of strength, courage, wisdom, and creativity."[2]

We shouldn't tell God how big our problems are; we should tell our problems how big our God is.

We shouldn't tell God how big our problems are; we should tell our problems how big our God is. We must remind the enemy that we claim all God's promises! Scripture assures, "God is our refuge and strength, an ever-present help in trouble. Therefore we will not fear" (Ps. 46:1–2).

Trust God's Character

My husband's frustration was palpable. He paced the office, muttering to no one in particular. "I don't get it. It makes no sense," he spewed as he walked by.

Our small office had lost two staff members, both resigning the same day. Neither one had left because they disliked their job. God simply had a new call for the next season of their lives. Both had been trusted, exemplary staff members. Both would be wished well and missed terribly, and both had left a big hole to fill. We never before had difficulty filling positions with qualified and eager candidates. This time, however, when we most needed help, it seemed impossible to find.

God knew our situation. My husband still endured chemotherapy treatments. I continued to care for him and our children while maintaining a busy private practice. Then I succumbed to a second bout of pneumonia in nine months. Stability was but an aspiration at that point.

I lamented to praying friends, "I don't understand what God is doing or why he doesn't intervene and provide." Crisis hit at every turn, completely beyond our control, leaving us desperate and wanting.

We trusted God as our source of help. Yet as time crawled, his help was neither quick nor obvious. My heart sank. I felt afraid, uncertain, doubtful, and even somewhat hurt. Our home and office were our mission field. How could we adequately serve others while our lives were in such disarray?

That morning neither of us felt well. My husband suffered side effects of his most recent chemotherapy treatment, and I had limited strength and stamina from the pneumonia. Yet we had an applicant to interview. That was worth venturing out to the office.

Thirty minutes before the interview, he received a text. "I woke up thirty minutes ago with allergies and bloodshot eyes. I won't be able to make it to the interview today."

Who cancels an interview for allergies and bloodshot eyes? A death in the family, we would understand. An ER visit, certainly. A flat tire, perhaps. But allergies and bloodshot eyes? Really?

My normally calm husband became "steamed" (his word) as he relayed the message. We both had hoped this was "the one"—God's provision for a dire situation.

My husband paced to release his frustration. I prayed simply, "Thank you, God, for revealing her nature and character before we made a hiring mistake." If one canceled an interview for bloodshot eyes, would they call in sick for a broken nail?

The situation wasn't what we had expected, nor was the outcome what we had hoped. But in such times, we must stay anchored to the reality of God's character. He knew we would face trouble, and he provided his peace despite the circumstances. "I have told you these things, so that in me you may have peace. In this world you will have trouble. But take heart! I have overcome the world" (John 16:33).

We felt lost, without answers or provision, but despite our troubling situation, we were not alone. God remained our refuge and provider (Ps. 46:1). My heart hurt, and I remained weary from the multiple battles we endured in recent months. Yet I took comfort in recognizing that sometimes God protects and provides as much by preventing things as in making or allowing them to happen.

We often don't understand why things occur. God's ways are frequently not our ways (Isa. 55:8–9). Yet we can trust God's character and recognize that he never withholds good from his children (Ps. 84:11). We can release our anxiety, knowing that he will do what is best, often protecting us from unseen harm. Even in times of trouble, we can rest in his gift of peace.

Know the Season Will Change

I donned my T-shirt, leggings, sweatshirt, and walking shoes. The sun shone brightly, the air still crisp as leaves and acorns crunched under my feet. All signs pointed to the promise of autumn, a welcome change from the summer heat. The change happened seemingly overnight. Really, it'd been coming for weeks. Days were shorter, nights were cooler, and the air-conditioning was less crucial. Yet if I hadn't been paying attention to these subtle signs, the seasonal change might have escaped me.

Summer had been blisteringly hot, warming the swimming pools and lakes to an uninviting temperature. I commonly heard the sentiment "I can't wait for fall to get here." It arrived, without any effort on our part but rather by an act of our Creator.

The year felt long, filled with trials and times that left us reeling. Each trial felt like an ocean surge crashing us against the rocks, leaving us beaten and bruised, wondering where it had come from and how we hadn't seen it coming. Fourteen weeks of pneumonia took me over six months to fully recover from. The death of a friend reminded us of life's fragility and the uncertainty of our numbered days. My husband's cancer diagnosis and treatment depleted the wind from our sails. Multiple staff members moved out of state, leaving my practice in flux and turmoil.

When trials hit and crises loom, they feel like an unforeseen natural disaster, leaving debris scattered in their wake. After a disaster, that's all we hear about on the news for days or weeks. The same thing happens in our lives after a crisis. Our attention is focused on the crashing waves of our thoughts threatening to pull us under. We long to escape unscathed, and we seek the return of some semblance of normalcy. Fervently, we try to pick up the broken pieces and wrap our arms around them in a meager attempt to hold them together—until one day when we awake and realize the season is changing and the apex of the crisis has passed. We sit in a new normal, survivors, even if a bit battered and bruised.

Our Creator causes the seasons to change, and he is the One who brings our attention to the changing of the seasons. He says, in a way, "See, you are coming through it." He deserves our praise. He remains the author and finisher of our faith, the One who will cause all things to work together for our good and for his glory.

Peace despite Crises

When crises hit and chaos assaults, either we can choose to trust the facts of our circumstances or we can trust God's promises. Isaiah 26:3–4 reveals how our peace (or lack thereof) depends on the choices we make. "The steadfast of mind You will keep in perfect peace, because he trusts in You. Trust in the LORD forever, for in GOD the LORD, we have an everlasting Rock" (NASB).

In Hebrew, "steadfast" means "to lean, to rest, to support."[3] It's the notion of being held up as we lean on something. "Of mind" means "to frame" or "to fashion, to form," as in frame of mind.[4] Altogether, in essence, "steadfast of mind" means "a frame of mind that one is upheld and supported while leaning on something." The verb "will keep" means "to guard from danger, to watch over."[5] God is the Rock on which we can lean. While we are upheld and supported by leaning on God our Rock, he also watches over us, guards us from danger, and keeps us in his peace as we trust him. Essentially, we must choose to discard every support we tend to rely on and give all our worry, anxiety, and fear to the only One who can support us with his strength.

Can you imagine maintaining a calm, restful mind in spite of your circumstances? I experienced such a choice. Following the Christmas holiday, I returned to my private practice ready for the new year. I looked at our upcoming schedule and was shocked to see a lighter caseload than my first year in business. Staring at the computer monitor, I mentally asked a plethora of questions: Why is the calendar so empty? How will we pay the mortgage? And our staff? How long can we keep the doors open in this current state?

Immediately after the barrage of questions flooded my mind, I determined to declare truth. "This has been God's practice since our first day in business. God has always met our needs, and he will continue to do so. Don't let this steal your peace. Trust God and lean on him to be the strength that supports you through this lean time."

By purposely trusting God, I transferred the responsibility for the outcome onto his broad shoulders. When I offered him the situation and the potential worries surrounding it, I rested in his peace. None of this took him by surprise, and he would have the perfect solution for my perceived problems.

Strong winds make flight difficult for many birds. For eagles, though, strong winds are an aid to flight. The eagle's wings are designed to catch updrafts and allow the bird to gain altitude and travel long distances without having to expend the energy to flap their wings, especially useful as they migrate. They use what some would consider adversity to their advantage.[6] This is a lesson for us. When storms come, we need to rely on God's help to soar beyond them, using the winds that usher in turmoil to carry us through them.

If you are troubled, don't consent to worry. Trust God, who is mighty to save. "But I call to God, and the LORD will save me" (Ps. 55:16 ESV). He wants to wipe away every tear. He longs to mend every broken heart. He desires to guide along every concerning path. He calls us to trust rather than to worry, fear, and fret. He is the ultimate answer in any crisis.

Your Rx

1. Look up the following verses: Psalm 46:1–2; John 16:33; 2 Corinthians 4:8–9; and 1 John 4:4. Then write them on index cards and place them where you will see them frequently. Read each of these passages aloud three times daily, committing them to memory.

2. Pray and ask God what beliefs you maintain that need to be changed so that when a crisis hits, you have the truth-based beliefs, attitude, and mind-set you need to weather any storm.

3. Consider times when you have experienced God's faithfulness. Record these times somewhere you can quickly reference them as a reminder during times of crisis.

My Prayer for You

Father, I lift up each one who is facing a time of crisis right now. We know that you see the end from the beginning and already have a plan to rescue and save. I ask that in your divine mercy you give your presence, protection, and provision for every need and that you turn every aching heart toward you to reap a greater measure of trust in you. You are our shelter and strength, always ready to help in times of trouble. We come to you, confident that you will do as you promise, that you are ready and willing to supply every need according to your glorious riches. We thank you in advance for your awesome deeds. In Jesus's name, amen.

Recommended Playlist

"Faithful," Gateway Music, © 2018 by Gateway Music

"In Jesus' Name," Darlene Zschech, © 2015 by Integrity Music

"Broken Hallelujah," The Afters, © 2013 by FairTrade/ Columbia

"I Am," Crowder, © 2014 by sixstepsrecords / Sparrow Records

"Eye of the Storm," Ryan Stevenson, © 2015 by Gotee Records

"Even Then," Micah Tyler, ℗ 2017, 2016 by Fair Trade Services

"Perfect Peace," Laura Story, ℗ 2008 by Laura Story

7

Say No to Worry, Anxiety, and Fear

Do not be afraid—I am with you!
I am your God—let nothing terrify you!
I will make you strong and help you;
I will protect you and save you.

Isaiah 41:10 GNT

Nothing in the affairs of men is worthy of great anxiety.

Plato

God's perspective on worry, anxiety, and fear is clear: he repeatedly says do not worry, be anxious, or fear. In Isaiah 43:5, he instructed, "Fear not, for I am with you" (ESV). We should not fear or become anxious because he is with us and is our strength, protection, and provision (Isa. 41:10). Matthew 10:31 tells us not to be afraid and emphasizes that we are far more valuable to him than sparrows.

God knows that worry, anxiety, and fear are counterproductive to our physical health, our emotional well-being, and our relationship with him. His instruction to "fear not" underscores that worry, anxiety, and fear cannot be tolerated as the norm. Instead, we must look to him for help in fear-festering situations. The Word clearly says, "Do not be afraid."

His instruction to "fear not" underscores that worry, anxiety, and fear cannot be tolerated as the norm.

So, practically, how do we do that? We don't like being weighed down by worry, anxiety, and fear, and yet we still are. I have recently taken a new approach to the things that tempt me to entertain worry, anxiety, and fear. Now when I identify something that triggers them, I recite out loud, "That's God's job, and he is already taking control of that!" Then I picture myself laying my concern at his feet and leaving it there for him to pick up and handle.

Trust Comes First

We cannot say no to worry, anxiety, and fear until we decide that we will trust God.

"Trust in the LORD with all your heart . . ." (Prov. 3:5).

All my heart? *Every* bit? The scary places? The parts of me I don't let others see? The parts that I don't like to acknowledge: Insecurities? Fears? Finances? Relationships? Decisions? My future? My past? Trust him that good could actually come from my past?

It's a tall order to trust the Lord with *all* your heart.

"and lean not on your own understanding . . ." (v. 5).

If I'm honest with myself, you, and God, I don't have it all figured out. But I try. From childhood, I possessed a very independent spirit. I was a problem solver, a doer, a go-getter, an achiever. "Try, try, try again until you figure it out" was my motto.

The problem? That's not biblical. It left no room for "lean not on your own understanding." In the last several years, God has had to break the wild stallion in me—not out of anger but rather out of love.

Leaning on our own understanding is a very lonely, isolating, exhausting, and fearful place to be. What if we're wrong? Frequently, I was. Scripture says, "My people are destroyed from lack of knowledge" (Hosea 4:6). My soul was perishing because I needed to relinquish the pressure of relying on my own knowledge and trust him. Trusting God brings freedom. Relying not on our own understanding means trusting God rather than carrying the weight of the responsibility on our shoulders.

"in all your ways submit to him . . ." (v. 6).

All my ways? It always comes back to that, doesn't it? *All.* God never tolerates halfway. He never settles for halfhearted. He asks us to give all. Be all. Do all for him.

I didn't need him to search my heart on this issue. I knew the answer to the unasked question: there were some areas I had not submitted wholly to him.

Why? Fear. Rebellion. Blindness. Doubt.

Until we recognize and acknowledge our situation, we will stay stuck right where we are. And we will continue going around and around this same lesson, just as the Israelites did waiting to enter the promised land, until we submit to him in *all* our ways.

"and he will make your paths straight" (v. 6).

How often do we traverse the crooked path because of our own fear or lack of trust? The problem: slow or hesitant obedience is disobedience and results in pain.

In my journey to trust God more intentionally, I realized, and he confirmed in this verse, that he often requires something from us *before* he acts. I had to learn to trust first, submit to him and his ways, and *then* he would show me my path. Trust comes first.

The Most Important Thing You Can Do

I remember a time when several friends and loved ones were enduring terrible crises and I had no answers to offer them. I was tempted to worry. On my knees and on my face before the Lord, tears streamed. I could do nothing else. I could not:

- cure a family member's dementia
- reverse a coworker's divorce
- remove a relative's cancer diagnosis
- return a friend's imprisoned child
- overturn a friend's financial ruin

I petitioned God as my heart ached and my throat burned. I begged for answers, for some way I could help.

What do you do when a friend hurts and you have no answers?

Professionally, patients visit me for answers when they have exhausted other avenues. Frequently, I provide solutions others haven't. Yet in each of the above scenarios, I had no answers. The enemy of my soul wanted me to believe I was helpless. The fact remained that I did not know the answers, while the truth was that I had access to the One who has all the answers. The greatest gift we can give anyone is prayer and leading them to the One who not only knows their need but also knows how to meet their need. We may not have the answers for cancer, bankruptcy, infertility, or other life challenges, but we can trust the One who does.

Trust chooses faith over fear, confidence over cowardice, power over panic, dependence over independence, and anticipation over action.

Others say, and I have said, "I wish there were something more I could do other than pray." Friend, prayer is the most powerful gift we can offer anyone in need, and ourselves. But that gift requires the greatest amount of trust. Saying no to worry, anxiety, and fear requires such a trust. When we don't know what else to do, trust is the most important thing we can do. Trust chooses faith over fear, confidence over cowardice, power over panic, dependence over independence, and anticipation over action.

Be Anxious for No Thing

Dreams for my eldest son's future seemed to evaporate before our eyes, despite his diligence and hard work. As a family, we prayed together, discussed, made game plans and backup contingency plans. Yet the closer we approached deadlines, the less certain we felt the plans would work in his favor.

"Mom, I've never experienced anything like this. I've never given something my all and not succeeded and cost my loved ones significantly. I'm not sure what to do." Quite a lesson for an eighteen-year-old.

My husband and I problem-solved solutions, but each proved unfeasible. I asked several close friends to pray. One morning as I poured out my frustration before the Lord, I sensed him whisper to my heart, "What part of 'be anxious for nothing' do you struggle with?"

"Pretty much all of it, if I'm honest. You tell us to be anxious for *no* thing, yet it seems like *every* thing causes me to worry and fret right now."

God always points directly to the heart of the matter. In his question, he showed me not only that I had given in to the spirit of worry, anxiety, and fear about my son's future but also that it had unknowingly crept into other areas too.

How will I complete all my work prior to traveling and not be behind when I return?

What if my youngest son struggles to make friends and doesn't adjust well to high school?

When we meet with the oncologist, what will the scans reveal?

The longer I sat in the morning stillness, the more I realized that if I didn't intentionally give my concerns to God in prayer, I would sacrifice all peace while anxiety ran amok from one area of my life to another. Yet if I left my concerns with him, trusted him, and thanked him in advance for his answers in his perfect time and perfect way, my heart and mind would rest in his perfect peace. "Be anxious for nothing, but in everything by prayer and supplication with thanksgiving let your requests be made known to God. And the peace of God, which surpasses all comprehension, will guard your hearts and your minds in Christ Jesus" (Phil. 4:6–7 NASB). We need to remember to pray more and worry less.

Anxiety regarding my oldest son's future accomplished nothing except robbing us of peace during our time together. So we did all we could; he did all he was responsible for doing. Then instead of fretting and worrying, we trusted God's plan, that he would make a way where there seemed no way. If he didn't, we would still trust that he makes all things work out for our benefit (Rom. 8:28). Either way, we would win, and we would do so in peace.

Sue discovered the same principle:

> Humble submission to God's will was my only hope. After hundreds of hours in prayer, worship, and Scripture reading, I finally said, "God, I accept what has happened. I trust you will use it for my good and your glory." That moment of acceptance, giving up self-will to trust God knows best, brought a breakthrough.
>
> I no longer deal with anxiety. I refuse to engage it. I don't need to fight; God won those battles for me. Scripture says, "Be anxious for nothing." His truth is that I am not an anxious person but God's beloved child. God doesn't intend for his children to live in anxiety and worry; they have no right in my life. After that experience, I learned to trust Christ, not my feelings.

Release It

"Release it. Just release. You've done the work, now release it and let God handle the outcome."

These words of wisdom from my friend Marilyn Meberg dripped from my head to my heart during my time at the beach with the Lord. I had gone there to get away and gain perspective, unsure of what I would hear, when she offered those much-needed words of advice. She didn't know all the chaos that was pummeling me from every side like a summer hurricane. She knew of only one situation that both of us were powerless to influence.

There's nothing wrong with crying, but my upbringing did not tolerate tears. I learned to remain strong despite my pain. Now when I cry, I know one of two things is usually happening: either I'm truly at the end of myself, or the Lord is doing a deep work, or both.

From the moment Marilyn spoke, "Release," the tears flowed down my cheeks. The more she explained, the harder they cascaded until they were so fast and so thick I could no longer see the beach. It might as well have stormed on that beach because my heart felt dark and weighty like a storm. She wouldn't know until a subsequent conversation how her words spoke into several areas of my life, not just the original concern.

- Possible cancer? Release it. Cancer is a little *c*, Christ is a capital *C*. God trumps cancer.
- Possible financial ruin? Release it. God takes care of the sparrows. Surely he watches over you.
- Potential career change? Release it. God gave you your calling; he knows the good plans he has for you.
- A bullied child? Release it. He is God's child first, and God cares for him even more than you do.
- A child's uncertain future? Release it. You've trained your child up in the way he should go, and when he is old, he will not depart from it.

"Release it."

What does that mean anyway?

I knew. God reiterated the same thing during those few days as I walked with him along the beach, just in a different way: "I love you. Trust me."

Trust has always been difficult for me. Maybe it started when I was a toddler alone in the hospital or as a child when my father died. Maybe it was when my husband lost his job or when he received a cancer diagnosis. Somewhere I believed the enemy's lie that God wasn't trustworthy. But the One who created me was beckoning me back in tender love to trust him above all else.

Fear gives more credit to Satan's power than to God's.

Fear gives more credit to Satan's power than to God's. In my fear, I projected the enemy's lies onto my future and believed them. God challenged me to release my weighty concerns and trust what I couldn't see but what I knew to be truth: God is good, all the time.

Fear and faith both equally long to be expressed. We have a choice, but we can't choose both. One is from the enemy who seeks only to steal, kill, and destroy, while the other comes from our loving Father who desires only good for us, because he loves us. It's a choice. In order to say no to worry, anxiety, and fear, we have to release those cares into God's hands, trusting that he already knows how to intervene for our good and for his glory.

What do you need to release today and trust God for?

Let God Use Our Anxious Situations to Help Us Trust Him

Jesus instructed us, "So don't worry about tomorrow, for tomorrow will bring its own worries. Today's trouble is enough for today" (Matt. 6:34 NLT). If anyone ever had reason to worry about the future, it was Elijah and the widow at Zarephath in 1 Kings 17. Elijah prophesied a drought would last several years until he declared otherwise. Elijah could've worried, feared, and become anxious about his provision, but God hid him in the Kerith Ravine, where the brook provided water and ravens fed him.

I imagine Elijah became quite comfortable with the provisions God gave him, but the brook dried up and God directed him to Zarephath. When Elijah arrived, he asked a woman for water. As she went to fetch it for him, he called to her and also asked for a piece of bread.

The woman had been living in the drought conditions, and now a stranger asked her for provision she lacked even for herself. Elijah got on her last nerve. She barely had enough oil and flour to make one last meal for her and her son before they died, and Elijah not only asked for bread but also instructed her to make his first. This invoked worry, anxiety, and fear. Elijah instructed her not to be afraid but to go ahead and make a small loaf of bread for him and then another for her and her son. Elijah shared that God had told him she wouldn't run out of oil or flour until God returned rain to the land. The widow acquiesced and was rewarded daily with enough food for Elijah, herself, and her son, consistent with God's promise.

Despite daily provision for months, if not years, she still struggled to trust God's faithfulness and provision when a mother's worst fear was realized: her son became ill and died. She blamed Elijah and God.

Even Elijah, who had enjoyed a front-row seat for the miracles of food from ravens and a daily replenishment of oil and flour for him and the widow's family, seemed to grow a bit anxious at the dire situation. He stretched himself out three times on the boy, who lay lifeless on the bed, and prayed to God to revive the young lad. God heard Elijah's pleas and restored the boy's life. God not only brought the widow through her most anxiety-provoking life circumstances but also showed her that he was trustworthy. "She answered, 'Now I know that you are a man of God and that the LORD really speaks through you!'" (1 Kings 17:24 GNT).

Reflecting on times when we have seen God's goodness and faithfulness in the past, either toward us or toward others in difficult circumstances, can help us to trust God and say no to worry, anxiety, and fear in new circumstances. Seeing how God healed my husband from his first cancer diagnosis, for example, helped us to trust him and say no to worry, anxiety, and fear after his new diagnosis.

Linda's background made trust difficult:

> Raised in an alcoholic family, I learned early I couldn't depend on anyone to take care of me. My mother, suffering from anxiety and agoraphobia, rarely left home. She numbed her symptoms with prescription pills and alcohol. I learned to do the same. By the age of twenty-three, I couldn't leave home either. Panic attacks became my constant companion.
>
> But God. Those two simple but powerful words. When my brother committed suicide, I finally reached out to God. He was waiting for me. My healing wasn't instantaneous. But God met me in my pain and suffering. Learning his Word helped me through nightmarish days and eventually brought me to the other side.

Don't Give Worry a Voice

In my profession, I have noticed that people often offer what they believe to be a generally benign statement that really isn't. Frequently, people say, "I'm really worried that . . ." or "I'm afraid that . . ." then express their concern. What people often don't realize is that our words have power to speak life or death, blessings or curses to others and ourselves (Prov. 18:21). When we say, "I'm worried that . . ." or "I'm afraid that . . ." we give the enemy an invitation to inflict those things we are worried about or afraid of.

God commands us not to worry or to fear. He says, "Fear not!" and "Be anxious for nothing!" When we consider the vastness of God and his unwavering character, worry is not an option. He is bigger than anything we face. He holds the universe in one hand and our hands in his other. God never sweats the small stuff (to him, it's all small stuff). When we trust him, we don't have to sweat it either.

In *Hope Prevails*, I discussed reclaiming the peace our enemy tries to kill. One way he kills our peace is by invoking worry, anxiety, and fear. We often let him with our own words. Instead, we must trust God and focus on him to maintain our peace (Isa. 26:3). For example, instead of saying, "I'm worried I won't be able to make ends meet," exert your trust in God and declare, "God, I'm trusting you to provide because you promise to supply all my needs according to your glorious riches." Or instead of saying, "I'm afraid to be alone," look to his promises and declare your trust in him: "Thank you, God, that you promise you will never leave me and will always be with me so I won't be alone."

Rather than worrying or being anxious or afraid of something, we need to think about God. He already has our circumstances figured out. We must carefully choose our words. Our words have the power to bring peace or worry, anxiety, and fear into a situation. We should speak powerful, life-giving words into our situations and over our loved ones. We must keep our thoughts firmly planted on God, and then we will stay in his peace.

Be Boldly Courageous

"Boldly courageous." God gave me that phrase to live by one year. It sounded exciting at first—like a warrior princess, adventurous and brave. I didn't anticipate what it would entail.

Being boldly courageous meant going where I was afraid to go, doing what I was afraid to do, being brave when I was afraid, confronting the spirit of fear and declaring him defeated even when my circumstances suggested otherwise. It meant trusting when I was tempted with worry, anxiety, and fear. It meant setting off into unknown waters, trusting I wouldn't sink. Ultimately, it meant trusting the One who sent me, trusting he would never leave me or forsake me (Deut. 31:8), trusting he would finish the work in me that he had started (Phil. 1:6), trusting his plans for me were good and would prosper and not harm me (Jer. 29:11).

Circumstances repeatedly challenged me. My gut said, "No way!" but my heart knew I must say, "Yes" in obedience to what God called me to do. As I fought

> *He doesn't call us to have the answers, but he calls us to surrender and trust.*

between the two, my husband would remind me, "This is what boldly courageous looks and feels like!"

Conversations required me to go deeper than I felt comfortable with, sharing more vulnerably than I preferred to. Situations occurred requiring me to step outside my comfort zone when I preferred to stay nestled in the familiar.

I had a choice: shrink back in fear and wonder what could have been or be boldly courageous, trusting God because he and his plans for me are always good. I chose courage and trusted God for my spouse's health, our finances, my children's well-being, and our business staffing needs.

We know who is able and who holds the future in his hands. He doesn't call us to have the answers, but he calls us to surrender and trust.

Remember God Is Our Source of Peace

Early in my Christian walk, I recognized God as my only source of hope, consistent with Romans 15:13: "May the God of hope fill you with all joy and peace as you trust in him, so that you may overflow with hope by the power of the Holy Spirit." I couldn't understand how people coped in difficult times without a relationship with him. What hope did they possess? Clearly, they had none. I understood the first portion of that verse, yet I longed for the next portion: "fill you with all joy and peace."

Sometimes I wish God would write his instruction on the wall for us. I remember a time when it might have helped if he had written "Trust me" on the wall to confirm what I sensed in my heart. I couldn't ignore his question: "Do you trust me, Michelle?" Tears cascaded down my perfectly made-up, ready-for-work face.

I needed to get real with God; there hardly seemed time. Patients were scheduled within the hour, and this was not exactly a neat and tidy issue that could be discussed in the length of a Snapchat or a Twitter post.

"I want to, Lord," I cried.

"Yes, but . . ."

"You know . . ." Tears flowed harder now (just what I didn't want to happen).

"Tell me," he encouraged.

"I trust you in some things."

"But . . ."

I wept, and my heart rate accelerated, knowing I couldn't avoid the issue any longer. "But I'm afraid."

In my seeking, searching, and fervent prayer, God led me to Romans 15:13: "May the God of hope fill you with all joy and peace *as you trust in him*, so that you may overflow with hope by the power of the Holy Spirit" (emphasis added). Frequently, God's interaction with us seems like an algebraic if-then equation. God is our only reliable source of hope, joy, and peace, but he cannot fulfill his end of the equation *until* we first trust in him.

The very things I longed for, prayed for, are ours for the asking and the receiving *if* and *because* we trust in him. Without trust, the rest of that verse is negated. We have hope, joy, and peace only when we trust in him; we must do our part first.

God asks us to give him all our concerns because the burden is too heavy for us to shoulder. He wants to carry the load, out of love and care for us (1 Pet. 5:7). We often hold onto our worries, fears, and anxieties like a security blanket, unsure how to survive without them. Rest assured, God has a better way: He will sustain us in his peace and won't let us crumble. "Cast your cares on the Lord and he will sustain you; he will never let the righteous be shaken" (Ps. 55:22).

I heard a story about a father and his daughter. While shopping with her mother, the little girl begged her mother to buy her a cheap dime-store pearl necklace. Her mother did, and every day that little girl completed chores to earn money to repay her mother for her prized possession. She wore the necklace everywhere she went: to kindergarten, running errands with her mother, even to bed. The only time she didn't wear it was in the bathtub; her mother warned her it might turn her neck green. One night as her father read her a bedtime story, he asked her to give him the pearls. She replied, "Oh, Daddy, you know I love you. I'd give you anything, just not my pearls. How about my sweet, beautiful doll?"

"No, honey, that's okay. I love you." He kissed her good night and turned out the light.

This happened nightly until finally one night the father came in to read a story only to find his daughter on the bed with her lower lip aquiver.

"What's wrong, honey?" Without a word, she handed her pearls to him. At that, the father reached into his coat pocket and pulled out a small blue velvet box and handed it to her.

"What's this, Daddy?"

"Open it, honey." She opened the box and inside was a beautiful strand of genuine pearls. The father had waited for her to be willing to give up her junk in exchange for true treasure.

I wonder just how often our heavenly Father waits for us to give up our junk that doesn't serve us well in exchange for his good and perfect gifts. *When* we give him our worries, fears, and anxieties, trusting he knows best how to handle what concerns us, *then* we are freed to receive his hope, joy, and peace.

Trust Him in the Storms

I don't live near the coast, but whenever I can, I go. God and I have an agreement: since he is gracious enough to paint the sunrise, I get up and appreciate the splendor, regardless of how early it happens.

On a family trip to the ocean, I set my alarm for o'dark-thirty, got up, and padded my way down to the surf. I toted my creature comforts: towel, coffee mug, and camera.

That morning as I sat on the cool, damp sand, waiting expectantly for a beautiful burst of rainbow hues to explode over the horizon, storm clouds engulfed me, taking me by surprise. Off in the distance, I spotted the tiniest familiar glimmer of pink, while dark billows loomed overhead. As I waited patiently, one drop fell, then two. Within moments, the ominous storm clouds overhead pelted me with arrows from their quiver, cold and sharp.

Hints of God's splendor remained on the horizon while I sat beneath the storm. While I would not be witness to the sunrise's majesty that day, someone somewhere was surely viewing the glorious, heavenly pinks, oranges, and yellows of a new day.

Where was God in my storm?

As the rain fell, soaking me through my towel and my clothing, my heart felt cold and damp too. Recent events had me feeling left out in the rain and wondering where God was in my personal storms. But as I had journeyed through those storms, I had learned a few things.

- Sometimes God calms the storm before it causes destruction.
- Sometimes he waits for us to come to him in the midst of the storm.
- Sometimes he waits out the storm with us to prove that he never leaves us.

That stormy morning, just because I didn't see a magnificent sunrise didn't mean God wasn't there. He was equally there in the wind and the waves, in the dark clouds and the rain. With one word, he created them, and with one word, he could silence them.

He was no less present or less powerful in the storm than in a peaceful sunrise. The question is, will we trust him in the storm and be thankful regardless?

Tomorrow is a new day and a new sunrise. We must be intentional about not missing out on the blessings and the lessons he has for us today, even in the midst of the storm.

Remember Who Your Father Is

After arriving home from a hectic speaking and travel schedule, I needed to regain some semblance of peace. Taking some time away from my to-do list and spending some time on the water usually accomplishes that for me. On the water, laundry doesn't beckon me, grocery lists are forgotten, cell service is poor, and nobody can reach me. For a few moments, I can enjoy peace and solitude, uninterrupted by people or projects. So my husband and I threw towels and sunscreen into a bag and headed to the lake. We took a boat out for a few hours to relax on the water and reconnect with each other and with God.

While we were on the water, the weather turned without warning. The wind whipped up, and the waves violently tossed our craft beyond our control. Steering the boat proved all but impossible as the bow beat against one wave after another. The fierce journey left me sick and queasy.

I recalled when Jesus was out on the water in a boat with his disciples (Matt. 8:23–27). While they were out there, a fierce storm brewed as Jesus slept soundly. While he slept, the disciples got themselves in a dither because they were afraid. They awoke him, saying, "Lord, save us! We're going to drown!" (Matt. 8:25). Mark 4:38 puts it bluntly, "Teacher, don't you care if we drown?"

I don't know what storm you face. I've experienced many in recent years. We all experience them, either physically or figuratively. The Bible warns we will go through trials, but it also encourages us to take heart because Jesus overcame the world (John 16:33).

I pondered how Jesus could sleep through that storm. Perhaps Jesus slept because he knew who his Father was. He trusted his Father to take care of him. Whatever Jesus did, he always tended to his Father's business. As a result, he trusted his Father to care for all his needs. Just as Jesus did, remembering who our Father is and how much he loves and cares about us can help us say no to worry, anxiety, and fear and maintain our peace even in the midst of our storms.

Whatever storm you are enduring right now, it doesn't surprise God. God isn't wringing his hands in heaven, wondering, *How could this have happened? How can I protect my child through this?* Your heavenly Father knows your storm, and he's going to see you through it to the other side.

Your Rx

1. Look up the following verses: Proverbs 3:5–6; Isaiah 41:10; and Philippians 4:6–7. Then write them on index cards and place them where you will see them frequently. Read each of these passages aloud three times daily, committing them to memory.

2. Romans 15:13 explains that an exchange takes place. First we trust, then God grants his hope, joy, and peace. Where do you need to trust God as you wait for his hope, joy, and peace?

3. Consider the girl in the story with the necklace and reflect on what you've held on to that wasn't the best for you when God wanted to give you real treasure instead. Confess that now and surrender it to him.

My Prayer for You

Father God, many times in your Word you tell us, "Fear not," "Do not worry," and "Be anxious for nothing." Surely you knew we would all struggle with worry, anxiety, and fear or you wouldn't have repeatedly told us not to in Scripture. Father, I pray for the one reading these words right now that you would infuse peace into their heart in place of any worry, anxiety, or fear they might be experiencing. Let your heavenly peace, calm, and comfort replace all fear or dread. Grow their ability to trust in you for all things instead of worrying about their own limited capacity. I thank you for caring about everything that concerns us. Thank you for being our ultimate provider! In Jesus's name, amen.

Recommended Playlist

"Cast Your Burden," Gateway Music, © 2018 by Gateway Music

"Cast My Cares," Finding Favour, © 2015 by Gotee Records

"Praise You in This Storm," Casting Crowns, © 2005 by Reunion Records

"Take Courage," Kristene DiMarco, © 2017 by Bethel Music

"Sparrows," Jason Gray, © 2016 by Centricity Music

"Everything," Lauren Daigle, © 2018 by Centricity Music

8

God Is

And Gideon built an altar to the LORD there and named it Yahweh-Shalom (which means "the LORD is peace").

Judges 6:24 NLT

Peace is not the absence of troubles but the presence of Christ.

Sheila Walsh

For many years, I considered things like joy and peace intangibles. That was my way of saying, "I can't see them, I can't touch them, and I can't even really understand what they are or how to get them." They both seemed like happy words from Christmas carols, foreign and yet appealing.

As I prayed for God's joy and peace to consume me, I realized the truth of Scripture that God *is* our peace. Peace is not a thing; peace is a person. "For he himself is our peace" (Eph. 2:14). We allow our daily experiences and the enemy's lies to cloud our vision and rob us of our peace, but "God is not a God of disorder but of peace" (1 Cor. 14:33 NLT), so we must trust him.

So often we put pressure on ourselves to do things, to get things right, to control an outcome. But we are in a partnership with a God who cheers us on, walks with us, and takes responsibility for the results. Our job is to be obedient to what he has told us to do, knowing his peaceful presence is with us. "Whatever you have learned or received or heard from me, or seen in me—put it into practice. And the God of peace will be with you" (Phil. 4:9).

> *There is no peace apart from God. He provides our peace and is our peace.*

In our spiritual walk, we all stumble and even fall. We make mistakes and sin. Yet the God of peace extends grace and consistently makes us more like him. "May God himself, the God of peace, sanctify you through and through" (1 Thess. 5:23). We must recognize that the world cannot provide peace. There is no peace apart from God. He provides our peace and *is* our peace. "They will be in awe and will tremble at the abundant prosperity and peace I provide" (Jer. 33:9).

God Is Able

During the middle of an otherwise normal day, my husband walked in on me writing patient reports. "Honey, we need to talk." I knew that tone, and it wasn't good. He went on to relay that he had been laid off from his job in telecom, leaving him unemployed and without health insurance. This was unexpected despite the unfortunate economic situation nationally. All of telecom moved out of the area, yet a move wasn't the answer for us because my private practice was stable.

The situation seemed impossible to me. We searched for answers, but in our humanness, we found none. Doubt and despair tempted us. I usually possess a take-charge personality. The problem was, I could do nothing but depend on God's intervention. My prayers were not elegant or eloquent. In desperation, I tearfully prayed, "Lord, please, we need help. Your ways are higher than ours. We trust you, Lord, and know you are able, but we need your help *now*."

Sometimes the wait for God to move feels unbearable. Type A personalities have to fight against the urge to "help" God. This trying time tested me but also taught me several things.

- There's nothing God can't do. When we feel brokenhearted and the circumstances seem impossible, he is able.
- Unlike people who let us down, God remains faithful. He can tame the raging sea within our hearts and move the highest mountain of our circumstances.

Despite the difficult circumstances:

- He was there in the middle of the trial (Ps. 5:11).
- The greatest sacrifice I could give was my praise and surrendering my desires to what he deemed best (Heb. 13:15).
- Whatever he does is better than I could have planned, asked for, or imagined (Eph. 3:20).

Linda found this to be true as well:

> I can do nothing in my own strength to "fix" the problem. When I believe Jesus can do all things and release my concerns to him, my soul experiences peace and I can pray in faith, believing. Worshiping and praising Jesus, focusing on him, looking at what he is doing, and speaking his truth out loud help the most!

When we remember that God is able, it makes it easier to exchange our worry, anxiety, and fear for our worship of him.

Here is Carolyn's experience:

> When my teenage daughter became a prodigal, I knew I was in serious trouble. I drowned in depression's waters. My heart ached. I was the classic worrying mom, always

> needing to know she arrived safely at each destination. Now,
> I would never know. I knew I couldn't continue like that and
> had to entrust her to God. I realized God had control of it all
> along, but not until I feared for my peace of mind did I realize
> I should worship rather than worry. Each time she entered
> my thoughts, I praised the Lord, despite how I felt. I learned
> that worship is healing and crucial for peace.

When we face trials and when worry, anxiety, and fear threaten to overwhelm us, our best course of action is to remember God is our source of peace, submit our feelings to him, and trust his promises.

- He will never leave us nor abandon us (Deut. 31:6).
- We will never be alone (Deut. 31:8).
- He will work everything for our good (Rom. 8:28).
- No weapon formed against us will prevail (Isa. 54:17).
- What the enemy intended to harm us, God will use for good (Gen. 50:20).
- Those who trust in the Lord will not be disappointed (Isa. 49:23).
- He has a *good* plan for us (Jer. 29:11).

We must settle in our minds that God is who he says he is and will do what he says he will do. Regardless of our need, God is able!

God Is All We Need

Sleep had been insufficient the previous night. I arrived home from one trip, unpacked, washed laundry, and repacked for another trip. Tripping over the dog (who I think only had one eye open herself), I spilled coffee on my cream skirt as I dashed out the door for work.

Would my patients notice the coffee trail down my skirt?

Who was I kidding? I would notice it all day. But I had no time to change clothes. I had scheduled a double load of patients that day since I was attending a conference the remainder of the week.

I pulled out of the garage sharply, just missing the garbage by the curb. As I pressed the garage door opener, the garage door didn't come down, but my tears did.

"Lord, we aren't going to have a day like this today, are we?"

He swiftly answered in my spirit, "Are we? It's your choice."

"I suppose it is."

The tears rolled. They weren't about the dog, the coffee, or the garage door. They were about the major life stressors those minor incidents represented. "What you're really saying is I need to trust you, right?"

I pictured a heavenly nod and a fatherly smile, although I didn't smile; tears still flowed through my exhaustion and frustration. "What do you want me to trust you for, Lord?"

I sensed his reply. "What is it you need, child?"

I often prayed for others' needs more than my own, so I wasn't sure how to answer that question. What *did* I need?

I needed God to be my peace, my Jehovah Shalom.

I needed him to be my provider, my Jehovah Jireh.

I also needed him to fight my looming battles, to be my Jehovah Nissi, my battle fighter.

Was that all?

When people deserted me, I needed his presence as my Jehovah Shammah, the Ever Present One.

I am sinful and imperfect. I needed him to be my Jehovah Tsidkenu, my righteousness.

Feeling lost and needing direction, I needed him to be my Jehovah Rohi, my Good Shepherd.

"Anything else, child?"

In complete honesty (he knew anyway), I needed him to be my Jehovah Rapha, my healer.

In that early morning exchange, he showed me I can trust him to be all I need. Because he is the great I AM who is sufficient for all our needs, we have no reason to fear and every reason to trust. What is it that you need him to be for you right now?

God Is Our Provider

Recently, I looked at my office schedule and unconsciously spoke my surprise aloud. "What happened to the schedule? Where are all the patients?"

January often presents a somewhat lighter patient load with Christmas bills due and insurance deductibles restarting. Still, almost two decades after entering private practice, I saw a patient schedule lighter than ever, without explanation.

My initial inclination was panic. "We have bills to pay and staff who depend on the income. We have a son in college and another growing so fast I can't keep his stomach full."

I quickly course-corrected and declared, "I refuse to entertain the spirit of fear. This is the Lord's practice. He not only owns the cattle on a thousand hills but also owns all the hills. I choose to trust him to provide for our needs and to direct our course."

The next morning I felt drawn to the account of the rich young ruler. A man ran to Jesus and asked what he needed to do to inherit eternal life. Jesus summarized the commandments for him, to which the man defensively protested that he had kept all the commandments since childhood. Knowing his heart, Jesus explained that he needed to sell all his possessions, give to the poor, and follow Jesus. The man walked away sad and discouraged because he owned many possessions. Jesus declared to the disciples that it is difficult for the wealthy to get to heaven. To the confused disciples, Jesus explained, "It is easier for a camel to go through the eye of a needle than for a rich person to enter the kingdom of God" (Mark 10:25 ESV).

I considered the possible condition of the man's heart when Jesus answered him. He asked an earnest question, yet when Jesus answered, the man walked away unwilling to take the necessary actions to inherit eternal life. The payoff for his obedience would have been heavenly riches far greater than any earthly experience. I suspect his reluctance to make such an exchange stemmed from anxiety.

Perhaps he thought, *Acquiring these possessions took a lifetime. How will I ever regain what he's asking me to give away? What if I can't pay my bills? Where will I get food, shelter, or clothing? What about an emergency? What will others think? How can I know the cost will be worth it? I've obeyed every other command—why isn't that good enough?*

Honestly, I might have asked those same questions. I remember learning about tithing as a young girl. Every time I earned money babysitting or mowing neighbors' lawns, I gladly apportioned part to savings and part to a tithe. I tithe today. Yet I've heard others share that the more money they make, the harder tithing becomes. I wonder if they would rather make less money so it's easier to tithe a smaller amount. The root of the issue is fear of scarcity and lack and not trusting God's faithfulness to provide (not necessarily all we want but our true needs).

As I read the conversation between the man and Jesus, I noticed that every translation read, "Jesus loved him" or "Jesus felt a love for him." God doesn't impose rules because he is harsh or angry. He instructs us in the best way to live our lives because he loves us. Then out of our love and need for him, we trust him, we have faith in him, we praise him, and we thank him.

Jehovah Jireh means the God who provides. Because he promises to provide, we need nothing more to rest in peace. "I am convinced that my God will fully satisfy every need you have, for I have seen the abundant riches of glory revealed to me through the Anointed One, Jesus Christ!" (Phil. 4:19 TPT).

Do you see the key? God will meet *every* need. Not some, not a few . . . *every*. I don't know how or when, but I trust that he is already working everything out in his perfect way and his perfect time.

In our neediness, will we believe or will we let worry, anxiety, and fear rule our hearts? Perhaps we need to confess our unbelief to him and ask for an increased measure of faith.

God Is Greater

As I sit with my keyboard in my lap, my heart feels lodged in my throat. The number of emails, messages, and calls I recently received sharing burdens is almost too much for my empathic heart to bear.

Watching the news or glancing at social media for more than a few seconds yields horrific images of emergency responders rescuing people from the devastating consequences of Mother Nature's fury all over the world, while forecasters unsuccessfully attempt to predict the next storm's path.

I don't know what challenges confront you right now personally—the ravages of natural disasters, prodigal children, health emergencies, financial crises, relationship tension, or something else. The hot buttons for our family right now are health concerns, employment issues, family in the direct path of hurricanes, and more. But God is greater than it all!

Let's band together and unite our faith as a body of believers, believing God is bigger than what we see, bigger than what we feel, bigger than what we hear on the news. He created the universe, and he can still a storm, heal cancer, and restore relationships and finances. Begin to thank him now *in faith* for what he is already doing.

God Is the Restorer of Peace

Have you ever experienced turmoil? When you had more questions than answers? When you needed to know God sees you and cares for your every need?

I camped there on a sweltering day in Texas. I felt weighed down by the oppressive heat and the questions in my soul. I'd spent the last couple days sequestered to write but had grown weary.

Would I get done on time?

Would I effectively convey my message?

Would I hear his words, not mine?

Would anyone be interested in what I had to say?

Many questions, few answers.

As I prayed, God reminded me, "Do not be afraid of them; the LORD your God himself will fight for you" (Deut. 3:22). Needing a scenery change, I took a walk, and God met me, as he faithfully does. I meandered down a path, encountering one pond after another, each beautiful in its own regard. Each one stilled my soul a bit more.

It was fitting that as I was writing about peace and contentment, the Lord led me to the place I am most peaceful: by the water. The situation reminded me of the old hymn, "When peace, like a river, attendeth my way . . ."[1] It did. Peace washed over me, leaving me refreshed for the tasks that day. As I stood by the water's edge, I let the peace from my serene encounter with God still my heart and mind.

I understood the familiar passage in a new and fresh way: "The LORD is my shepherd; I shall not want. He makes me lie down in green pastures. He leads me beside still waters. He restores my soul" (Ps. 23:1–3 ESV).

In a few quiet moments, God restored my soul as I reflected on how much he must love me to know my every need and lead me beside still waters to refresh me with his peace. As I turned back, the sun beating down on my summer-bronzed shoulders, the summer's heat made my brow sweat. Suddenly, like a breath of the Spirit, a soft breeze engulfed me, as if God whispered, "I'm here. I see you. I know what you need. Trust me. I am your peace." Thank you, Lord, for that gentle reminder.

Friend, I don't know what answers you seek, what doubts you have. But I know God is present and cares about your needs. He alone is able to meet you and your every need right where you are. Will you trust him? As you do, he will restore your peace.

God Is Enough

I'm a recovering perfectionist. I say "recovering" because I struggle to relinquish that tendency any way other than perfectly. Even as I disentangle myself from those inbred tendencies, I wonder, *Am I doing it well enough?*

For many, striving for perfection is an attempt to compensate for another weakness. Some fear not being good enough. Others attempt to secure acceptance, inclusion, or love. Still others react from guilt or feeling flawed and unworthy.

Pamela shared:

> I coped with worry, anxiety, and fear most of my life. As a child, I feared any negative attention yet constantly sought the praise of adults who would acknowledge me and my efforts to succeed. I coped by isolation (hiding in the woods near our home for hours or closeting myself away with a book) and tried to avoid punishment from my parents or grandfather.
>
> In my teens, I discovered that anger kept people from knowing I feared them. Rather than risk rejection, I projected a tough-girl image that brought me "status" with my peers. With adults, I did everything to the extreme and portrayed an air of extreme self-confidence and self-assurance. If anyone questioned me on this, I lashed out in anger and defensiveness so they would not see the real me.
>
> Overachieving helped me cope with underlying fear and anxiety during my career. I feared that the simplest errors would result in my termination. I began a daily intense physical workout routine as well, hoping to be so exhausted at night that I would sleep for more than my usual three hours. Occasionally, I engaged in self-destructive behavior to numb the anxiety and fear.

Most of my life, I proudly wore the label "perfectionist." I viewed it positively, as a goal all should attempt to obtain. If I was perfect, perhaps others would consider me dependable, reliable, and even desirable.

Eventually, circumstances overtook me via illness, and I was able to do very little at all, much less perfectly. Devastated, I couldn't accept imperfection from myself. If I couldn't accept an imperfect me, I reasoned that others surely wouldn't either. Sadly, some didn't.

Gratefully, God accepts us and all our imperfections. We are not perfect, but he is, and when he looks at us, he sees the perfection of his Son, Jesus. He sees us not as we are but as we are becoming—more like him.

While I grow and mature, I remain grateful that Scripture says we already have everything we need for living a godly life (2 Pet. 1:3). When we review the names of God and what they signify, we realize that he, in his perfection, is everything we need. And when we consider what Christ's death on Calvary accomplished, we are complete and lacking nothing in him. The question is, will we appropriate Christ's gift? Trust it? Will we remember who we are, whose we are, and what we have gained as a result?

> *He sees us not as we are but as we are becoming— more like him.*

God Is Trustworthy

"Don't talk to strangers." "Don't open the door when you don't know who is there." "Don't accept a ride from someone you don't know." We teach our children these lessons. The underlying message suggests, "Don't trust anyone; you must know their character first."

I recently conversed with a woman about this issue. She felt broken and wounded. She had trusted and been betrayed. Rejected and abandoned. Her trust radar had deceived her, and now she struggled to trust again, even in God. Understandably so.

"How do I know I can trust God? How do you know?" she asked simply, but her heart implored and her tears begged.

"Because the best predictor of future behavior is past behavior . . . even for God," I explained.

The Bible contains over 220 verses specifically about trusting God. If you are like most people, just telling you *about* something may not convince you to *do* something. When we teach children how to decide whom to trust, we teach them to assess someone's character to determine if they are trustworthy. Scripture reveals that God's character makes him trustworthy.

God is:

- not human and he cannot lie (Num. 23:19)
- righteous (Jer. 9:23–24)
- loving (John 3:16)
- caring (Matt. 6:26)
- compassionate (Ps. 103:4–5)
- understanding (Ps. 139:1–2)
- forgiving (Ps. 103:12)
- gracious toward us (Eph. 1:7–8)
- sovereign (Ps. 103:19)

Furthermore, God:

- shows loving-kindness (Ps. 86:15)
- pardons us (Ps. 103:3)
- redeems us (Job 19:25)
- renews us (Isa. 40:31)
- satisfies us (Ps. 107:9)
- knows us (Ps. 139:1–6)
- accepts us (Rom. 15:7)
- heals us (Isa. 53:5)

No human possesses all of these traits simultaneously, but God does. He has never failed me. He has proven himself trustworthy to me, and he will prove himself trustworthy to you if you allow him to. We can have peace rather than worry, anxiety, and fear because God, the giver of peace, is trustworthy.

God's Perfect Peace

I needed to get away for some quiet with God. The noise of the world clamored in, drowning out his still, small voice—the only voice that matters, the only voice that brings peace in the storm.

I messaged a friend, "A tidal wave of overwhelm just hit me. The car hunt yielded nothing, and we need a car this week. School resumes Monday. Monday and Wednesday will be spent at the hospital for my husband's PET scan, then surgery. I work Tuesday, Thursday, and Friday. My Tuesday night teaching needs preparation. My neck is spasming. I need rest. I need time with God." She offered to call, talk, even pray. But my heart longed for stillness, quiet, and God's voice.

Fear and anxiety can result in selfishness because we focus on ourselves and not others or God. Stress is mostly a self-inflicted wound. It isn't God's way. His grace is found in stillness with him. He commands, "Be still, and know that I am God!" (Ps. 46:10 NLT). He doesn't suggest, "Spin your wheels, fret, and try to do more."

"Peace: it does not mean to be in a place where there is no noise, trouble, or hard work. It means to be in the midst of all those things and still be calm in your heart."[2] I knew the prescription. I frequently offered it. I encouraged it in *Hope Prevails*. Whenever we face worry, anxiety, or fear, time in God's presence must always be a priority to maintain our peace. Trials are inevitable, but thankfully, Scripture encourages us that Jesus already overcame those trials. In the midst of those trials, we make a choice. We choose where to focus: either on the trial or on the One who helps us through the trial.

Remember our discussion regarding Jesus and Peter walking on the water in chapter 6? In the midst of life's storms, I am comforted by the passage, "But Jesus immediately said to them: 'Take courage! It is I. Don't be afraid'" (Matt. 14:27). Jesus didn't wait—he saw their need and immediately addressed them. In the midst of the storm, Jesus told Peter, "Come" (v. 29). Jesus was already waiting for Peter, and he is waiting for us too.

How often do we rush through the busyness of our day or get stuck in the middle of our storms, frantically searching for answers, when all along the best answer is getting away, answering his call to come, and spending a few minutes being still in his presence? Doing so doesn't remove the problem, but it shifts our focus from the problem to the Problem Solver. God's peace is not the calm after the storm. It is the steadfastness during the storm. It is in his presence that we can find peace in the midst of the storm.

Peace is positional. It depends on our relationship with God (Rom. 5:1–2). If we lack intimacy with God, our peace is impaired (Ps. 85:8; James 3:17), and we find ourselves in conflict with God. God extends to us the privilege of his presence (Heb. 4:16), but for it to be effective, we have to exercise that privilege. James 4:8 says, "Draw near to God, and he will draw near to you" (ESV). Peace comes from being aligned with our Creator (Rom. 8:6; 1 Cor. 14:33). We find peace in the quiet moments when our hearts release our brokenness and pain in order to inhale the fullness of rest in him (Ps. 55:16–18). Stormie Omartian said, "The key to finding freedom from fear is making God your dwelling place."[3] God himself is our peace (Eph. 2:14), so if we desire peace, we must reside within his presence.

> *God's peace is not the calm after the storm. It is the steadfastness during the storm.*

Peace is also present tense. Unlike faith and hope, which look to the future, peace is offered for today. In John 14:27, Jesus tells his disciples that he leaves his peace with them. Almost all the letters of the New Testament include an offering of peace from the author to the readers. Colossians describes how Jesus makes peace between God and all things (1:20) and goes on to command that the "peace of Christ rule in your hearts" (3:15). These verses are all written in the present tense. Peace is made for today.

God is our shalom peace, and Jesus is our source of peace. The world can never offer the peace that we find in him. Jesus offered peace to us as a gift. We appropriate that gift by spending time with him. "Abide in me, and I in you. As the branch cannot bear fruit by itself, unless it abides in the vine, neither can you, unless you abide in me" (John 15:4 ESV). The more we spend time with him, the more we receive his peace.

Your Rx

1. Look up the following verses: Deuteronomy 3:22; John 15:4; Ephesians 2:14; and Philippians 4:19. Then write them on index cards and place them where you will see them frequently. Read each of these passages aloud three times daily, committing them to memory.

2. Have you ever felt as if you weren't good enough? Pray and ask God to show you how he sees you. Ask him to help you see yourself as he does.

3. Scripture relays that God has already given us everything we need, but we must choose to accept his provision. In what areas do you need to trust God that his provision is sufficient? Ask God to help you trust and receive his provision.

My Prayer for You

Father, I thank you that you are our peace. You promise to go before us, to walk with us, and to come behind us, always holding us with your righteous right hand. Because you never leave us, we lack nothing, including your peace. Thank you for being all we need. Thank you for being greater than the enemy, greater than worry, anxiety, and fear. You have already given us everything we need to live a godly life. Help us to rely on you and your truth to refute the spirit of fear and to trust you in all things. You alone are worthy of our trust because you have proven yourself faithful. Help us to position ourselves under the safe feathers of your wings. In Jesus's name, amen.

Recommended Playlist

"Defender," Gateway Music, © 2018 by Gateway Music

"Greater," MercyMe, © 2014 by FairTrade/Columbia

"Greater Than," Gateway Music, © 2018 by Gateway Music

"I Lift My Hands," Chris Tomlin, ℗ 2010 by sixstepsrecords / Sparrow Records

"Chain Breaker," Zach Williams, ℗ 2016 by Provident Label Group LLC

"The Way," New Horizon, ℗ 2018 by Sparrow Records, Bowyer & Bow

"God Who Moves the Mountains," Corey Voss, © 2017 by Integrity Music

"All That I Need," Gateway Music, © 2018 by Gateway Music

9

Reclaim Your Power

And I heard a loud voice saying in heaven, Now is come salvation, and strength, and the kingdom of our God, and the power of his Christ: for the accuser of our brethren is cast down, which accused them before our God day and night.

Revelation 12:10 KJV

On the back of Satan's neck is a nail-scarred footprint.

C. S. Lewis

It's easy to get trapped in an earthly perspective, focusing on only what we can see. As a result, many of us plan for every contingency out of a false sense of control and security, believing somehow that if we plan for every possibility, we won't be taken off guard and perhaps the trial will never come. The enemy uses this perspective against us. He distracts us with the what-if worries and fears so that we take our minds off God, his will, his promises, and his truths and focus instead on what we perceive in our limited scope of vision to be true. Hence, Scripture cautions, "Set your minds on things above, not on earthly things" (Col. 3:2). Earthly things often serve as a counterfeit to what God declared as true.

"God hath not given us the spirit of fear; but of power, and of love, and of a sound mind" (2 Tim. 1:7 KJV). God didn't give us a spirit of fear; instead he gave us three essential weapons to fight the spirit of fear.

First, he gave us power, the same power that raised Christ from the dead (Rom. 8:11). His power is our first weapon in the spiritual battle against worry, anxiety, and fear. In this chapter, we will delve into what it means to reclaim our God-given power.

He also gave us love, the same love that sent Jesus to die to erase our sins and allows us to spend eternity with him in heaven (John 3:16). In chapter 10, we will unpack this second spiritual weapon in our battle: living in Christ's perfect love.

Finally, he gave us a sound mind, the mind of Christ, which enabled him to walk in perfect unity with God in spite of his human limitations and the trials of this world (1 Cor. 2:16). In chapter 11, we will highlight this third weapon in our arsenal: utilizing our sound mind, which God gave us when he instilled in us the mind of Christ.

In order to live in his peace, free from worry, anxiety, and fear, we must first learn how to appropriate his power.

The search for peace is not as elusive as it sounds; we're not looking for the pot of gold at the end of the rainbow or a four-leaf clover in a grassy meadow. God desires for us to live in peace.

In Ezekiel 34:25–31, God promised to make a covenant of peace with his people, specifically to provide safety and blessing, security, freedom, prosperity, provision, lack of fear, and respect from their neighbors. Then they would know they were God's people and he was their Lord. He wants the same for us as well.

We become blinded by life's possible dangers, the potential lack of rain in our land, crops in our fields, resources in our cupboards. We believe the lies that have enslaved us. An ominous shadow engulfs us and conveniently blocks out both the Father and the Son and their many promises, their guarantees of safety and provision. We must determine our focus: what we see in the world or what we know and believe by faith because of God's supernatural promises. "Do not be afraid . . . for your Father has been pleased to give you the kingdom" (Luke 12:32).

Linda shared:

> Fear and anxiety bombard me when I assume responsibility for others' lives. I lose my peace when I watch my adult children and adult grandchildren make choices that result in negative consequences. I worry less during the day when I focus on Jesus and his Word, pray in the Spirit, and keep busy. Bedtime is the hardest. My mind races and fixates on what I did or what I should do now. I spiral downward if I lose sleep, am tired the next day, and feel paralyzed, unable to accomplish what I need to.

God declared that he did not give us the spirit of fear but instead power, love, and a sound mind. In order to live in his peace, free from worry, anxiety, and fear, we must first learn how to appropriate his power.

Power from Our Words

My patient studied my face as I explained, "I'm worried that . . . no, scratch that. I have a concern that if we don't address the issue, it could become more problematic later."

"Why did you say it like that?"

"Because our words have power, and God tells us not to worry. So I choose not to worry about this and to trust God while taking appropriate action."

She looked at me with a puzzled expression, the wheels turning inside her mind but the gears not fully engaging. She needed further explanation. "The Bible tells us repeatedly not to worry or be anxious and not to fear. God explains he has not given us the spirit of fear; instead, he gave us power, love, and a sound mind. In those situations when the enemy tempts us to fear, we can choose in our sound mind to trust that God loves us and will work in the situation for our good and for his glory. So while we may have concern, we don't need to worry or fear because we trust him for the outcome."

The Bible says that the words we speak contain great power. Our words have the power to give life or bring death (Prov. 18:21) and to bring blessing or cursing (James 3:10). So we can use our words to break anxiety's grip. For example, instead of saying, "I am afraid that the paycheck will run out before the bills are paid," we can say, "I choose to trust God to provide for all my needs just as he said he would."

Power from Speaking God's Word

We must be warriors, not worriers. God's armor is a key source of power in battling the spirit of worry, anxiety, and fear. "Put on the full armor of God, so that you can take your stand against the devil's schemes" (Eph. 6:11). Ephesians 6:17 says, "Take . . . the sword of the Spirit, which is the word of God." We speak from a place of power when we speak God's Word. Think about it: it's the same power (his words) which created an entire universe.

Reciting Scripture is the most important and most beneficial approach to combating worry, anxiety, and fear. The enemy whispers lies to entice us to acquiesce to fear. But we can use the truths of God's Word to defeat the enemy's lies. God promises that his Word will be productive for accomplishing his purposes, and part of that purpose is to defeat our enemy.

When I journeyed through the dark night of my soul, I participated in therapy, tried medication, ate a balanced diet, exercised, and made rest a priority. However, none of that impacted me as positively as reciting Scripture. I stuck favorite verses on my mirror, then on my nightstand, then on my closet door, bedroom door, and dashboard. Before I removed them, I had over one hundred verses posted where I would see them often. They both encouraged me in the moment and lodged their way into my memory for future direction and encouragement.

God promises, "As the rain and the snow come down from heaven, and do not return to it without watering the earth and making it bud and flourish . . . so is my word that goes out from my mouth: It will not return to me empty, but will accomplish what I desire and achieve the purpose for which I sent it" (Isa. 55:10–11). Romans 10:17 says, "Faith cometh by hearing, and hearing by the word of God" (KJV). God promised that his Word, even spoken by us, yields results.

Debbie shared:

> I battle back with the truth by reading God's Word and proclaiming it out loud so I hear it. I reach out to others for encouragement and allow them to speak truth. I quote Scripture and post these truths around my home. I repeat until I get the truths into my heart so that the seeds of trust, peace, and hope can take root and grow.

As I fought the spirit of fear, Psalm 91 gave me strength. I personalized it and applied it to my life so that it became more than words on a page; it became power in my soul. Let me give you an example with the first few verses:

When Michelle lives in the shelter of the Most High,
  Michelle will find rest in the shadow of the Almighty. . . .
He alone is Michelle's refuge, Michelle's place of safety;
  He is Michelle's God, and Michelle trusts him.
He will rescue Michelle . . .
  and protect Michelle.
He will cover Michelle. . . .
  He will shelter Michelle. . . .
Michelle will not be afraid of the terrors of the night,
  nor the arrow that flies in the day.

Ps. 91:1–5 NLT paraphrased

Often, before God intervenes in a situation, he waits for us to act. Verse 1 essentially says, "If _____ [insert your name here] will live in God's presence, *then* _____ will find rest and protection in his presence." We must first commit to living in, not just visiting, God's presence. We cannot rest safely outside his presence.

Every time we listen to the enemy, we step outside the safety of God's shelter and no longer rest in his peace. This is what the enemy sounds like:

"You can't possibly get everything done that needs to get done."

"You're going to let people down."

"You're in over your head."

"You can't trust anyone else."

"You will fail."

"The challenge is too big for you."

"There's nothing you can do."

When we accept what God has promised as ours, we are empowered for battle. Just as Jesus answered the devil in the wilderness with "It is written . . ." so should we use the power of God's Word to battle against worry, anxiety, and fear.

Verse 2 puts a stake in the ground, determining that God alone is our safe place, the only One worthy of our trust. When we trust him as our refuge, he promises in verses 3 and 4 that he will rescue us from every trap set for us, protect us from deadly diseases designed to kill us, and hide us under his sheltering wings where we cannot be open prey.

Verses 5–7 explain that when we trust God, we won't fear what *could* happen outside his safety, whether physical attacks on our body or the area around us, because God promises safety from such evil things.

Get excited and praise God that verses 8–13 reveal the great power that results from putting *all* our trust in him. That is crucial. We can't trust God and remain worried, anxious, or afraid about things. Scripture refers to that as being "double-minded." "He is a double-minded man, unstable in all his ways" (James 1:8 ESV). We must determine to fully trust God and his promises. When fear tempts, we must refuse to buy what it sells. We must choose God's peace instead. In Psalm 91:8–13, God explains how evil will be punished for tormenting those who trust God. Yet when we choose to trust God to be our shelter, refuge, and safe place, evil loses and anxiety is like cockroaches under the heels of our boots!

The last three verses of Psalm 91 promise God's rescue and protection when we love God and trust him fully. He promises to answer whenever we call in troubled times and bless us with long life despite the enemy's attempt to steal, kill, and destroy (John 10:10).

When we choose to trust God's Word and use its power to resist the enemy, the enemy has to leave (James 4:7–8). We refute the enemy's lies by speaking God's truth, which then removes us from the enemy's influence and keeps us safe in God's peace and protective care. When we draw near to God by reading and speaking his Word, he promises to turn closer to us and embrace us in the fullness of his love, mercy, grace, safety, security, and protection. In his arms, we have nothing to fear.

Power from Jesus's Name

Just as our words have power, and we have power from God's Word, we also have power through the name of Jesus. No name is more powerful than Jesus. Jesus declared, "Whatever you ask in my name, this I will do, that the Father may be glorified in the Son" (John 14:13 ESV).

We observe the disciples' example to see what a gift we've been given to call upon the name of Jesus for help and the power to defeat irritants such as worry, anxiety, and fear in our lives. The disciples expressed their astonishment when they declared, "Lord, even the demons submit to us in your name" (Luke 10:17). Can you imagine what would happen if we approached our daily lives with the confidence that because of Jesus's shed blood and the power and authority of his name, we can live in victory from anxiety?

The name of Jesus has the power to comfort, heal, bring peace, redeem, and save (Rom. 10:13). Worry, anxiety, and fear are not our portion. Holiness, peace, righteousness, and salvation are our portion because of Jesus. "He made you holy by means of Christ Jesus, just as he did for all people everywhere who call on the name of our Lord Jesus Christ, their Lord and ours" (1 Cor. 1:2 NLT). Jesus not only desires an eternal relationship with us in heaven, but he desires for us to live a peaceful, abundant life, unencumbered by worry, anxiety, and fear.

Cori-Leigh described:

> One night I was jarred from sleep, struggling to breathe! Another panic attack assailed me in my sleep. Knowing this was the spirit of fear, I called on the name of Jesus repeatedly in my mind. I lay on my bedroom floor, facedown, sobbing. There I surrendered all my burdens to Jesus: my childhood hurts, the pains and traumas of my past, and the years of being in bondage to my fears. He took it all as I laid it out before him. I got up four and a half hours later depleted emotionally, but I felt an inner peace I'd never experienced before. I was healed by his perfect love that casts out all fear. The anxieties and fears decreased, while peace, hope, and faith increased. Now he has given me peace in the midst of life's challenges and tragedies.

Power from Christ's Blood

Scripture tells us that we would do even greater works than Jesus did (John 14:12). That is possible only because Jesus gave us the perfect example to follow, then sacrificially died a criminal's death, shedding his blood on the cross before rising again three days later. "For in him all the fullness of God was pleased to dwell, and through him to reconcile to himself all things, whether on earth or in heaven, *making peace by the blood of his cross*" (Col. 1:19–20 ESV emphasis added).

Jesus shed his blood to defeat the enemy. "By his death he might break the power of him who holds the power of death—that is, the devil" (Heb. 2:14). The enemy thought he won when Jesus died on the cross. In actuality, Jesus set the stage for a perfect comeback! "The reason the Son of God appeared was to destroy the works of the devil" (1 John 3:8 ESV). Not only did Jesus defeat death, but his shed blood on the cross also powerfully defeated sin, shame, illness, worry, anxiety, fear, and every other weapon in the enemy's arsenal. "You were ransomed . . . with the precious blood of Christ, like that of a lamb without blemish or spot" (1 Pet. 1:18–19 ESV).

> *Not only did Jesus defeat death, but his shed blood on the cross also powerfully defeated sin, shame, illness, worry, anxiety, fear, and every other weapon in the enemy's arsenal.*

Jesus's blood broke the curse of sin, death, poverty, depression, and fear. In their place he loosed peace, joy, and hope found only through his sacrifice. The world can't offer lasting peace, joy, or hope. Scripture repeatedly tells us that Jesus came to give them to us. Jesus's empty tomb testifies to the power of his blood, while his resurrection proves Jesus is who he declared himself to be.

When the enemy taunts us with our sin and tries to make us worry, anxious, and fearful, we must remind him of the truth: the blood of the lamb cleansed us. "They have washed their robes and made them white in the blood of the Lamb" (Rev. 7:14). Jesus's shed blood defeated Satan, but he offers us that victory as well. "And they have defeated him by the blood of the Lamb and by their testimony" (Rev. 12:11 NLT). When we declare our trust in Jesus and praise him for all he has done and is doing, the enemy runs in fear of our power-packed words.

Power from God's Presence

Just as Jesus's name and Jesus's blood provide power, so does God's presence. Worry, anxiety, and fear result when we live outside the safe shelter of his presence. Peace dwells under the refuge of his shelter. We receive power by remaining in his presence. "Christ himself has brought peace to us. . . . Now all of us can come to the Father through the same Holy Spirit because of what Christ has done for us" (Eph. 2:14, 18 NLT).

After Jesus died, the women at his empty tomb mistakenly believed Jesus was no longer present with them, resulting in fear. The angel appeared to them, encouraged them to relinquish their fear, and assured them of his presence (Matt. 28:5–6).

Jesus also told them they had no reason to fear and assured them of his presence. "Then Jesus said to them, 'Don't be afraid!'" (v. 10 NLT). Jesus also promised them his continued presence: "And surely I am with you always, to the very end of the age" (v. 20).

When we look toward the Son, we never see our shadow—no worry, fear, anxiety, dread, shame, or past hurts. Because God is our peace and Jesus came to give us peace, we cannot possess peace apart from his presence. That is where we reclaim our power over the spirit of worry, anxiety, and fear. When we remain mindful of the presence of Jesus, we stay protected in his perfect peace.

Power from Believing God Will Answer Prayer

Sometimes it's easy to pray but with a seed of doubt. Sometimes we pray wondering, *Is God really going to answer?* Prayer is a powerful weapon that paralyzes the enemy. He attempts to limit our prayer time because he is fully aware that our prayers limit him.

Psalm 17:6 challenged me about how I pray. It says, "I am praying to you because I know you will answer, O God" (NLT). David prayed to God. He didn't get on social media or run to his friends for advice. He didn't ask his parents for their perspective or seek a pastor's wisdom. He took his needs straight to God. Why? Because he knew God *will answer*.

I love when Scripture says, "Will," because it offers confidence. It gives us reason to believe, reason to trust. It's a word marked with certainty, as in a promise.

I recently shared the many promises packed in Isaiah 61:1–3 with a congregation: God *will* comfort the brokenhearted; release the captives; free the prisoners; and exchange a beautiful crown for ashes, a joyous blessing for mourning, and festive praise for despair. Every time I came to the word *will*, I emphasized it because it offers another promise to claim and fills us with power, knowing we can trust God to fulfill his promises. Every time he says, "Will," we can count on it!

Psalm 17:6 promises that God *will* answer our prayers. How often do we pray really believing and knowing that God will answer—not hoping, not wondering but knowing? Worry, anxiety, and fear would cease if we continually refuted the enemy's lies with the confident assurance that God will answer our prayers.

> *Worry, anxiety, and fear would cease if we continually refuted the enemy's lies with the confident assurance that God will answer our prayers.*

I challenge you to go to him with your needs first; go to him before you go to your friends, parents, pastor, or counselor. Before you post on social media, pray. Before you turn the lights on in the morning, pray to God, knowing he will answer.

But don't put him in a box. Don't tell him how he must answer your prayer. However he chooses to answer, whenever he answers, know that he will provide the best answer for you, for your circumstances, and for his glory.

My friend April shared her experience:

> I was the anesthesiologist when a pediatric patient underwent a routine tonsillectomy. While still in the operating room, after I removed his endotracheal tube, he went into

bronchospasm and his oxygen saturation dropped, but he responded to measures. A few minutes later, after surgery, I noticed his pupils were not equal and one was without a light response. My worst fear was brain damage because of hypoxia. I felt fear and knew in my heart that something was wrong. While holding the anesthesia face mask on the boy, I bowed my head, closed my eyes, and prayed. "God, help me, help this boy. Work a miracle in this boy, for your glory. You said if we ask in your name with faith you will give us what we ask for. Nothing is impossible for you. Father, I ask you for his life, for his brain. I declare health over this child with all my heart in the sweetest and powerful name of Jesus. Amen."

No sooner had I finished praying, with my eyes still closed, that the boy woke up, moving his arms and pushing the mask off his face. He sat up and talked to me. All I said was, "Thank you, God. You're powerful and wonderful. The glory be to you." Those minutes felt like eternity. I had a lot of fear. I saw my career destroyed, a boy with permanent brain damage, and a family destroyed. But the Word of God says there is no condemnation for those who believe in him. So I filled my heart with faith and asked God for a miracle. I saw the hand of God in that operating room!

Power from Seeking God

The radiation technician offered a comforting smile as I lay down on the cold, hard "bed." She calmly explained each step of the procedure, not knowing my professional background or my knowledge of the intricacies of the procedure. Nor did she know I needed the assurances as a patient rather than a doctor that day.

"I'm leaving you, but I'll hear you from behind the wall if you need anything. The machine will tell you when to breathe and when to hold your breath." Right then, I realized I had already been holding my breath for what seemed like days. Since my doctor had declared,

"We need to run more tests to understand what's causing your pain," I had held my breath . . . waiting.

The moment she left my side, I felt alone in that freezing, sterile room. Alone, but not really alone. God promised never to leave me. I knew that, but my soul longed to feel it too. I closed my eyes, trying not to think of the several possible diagnoses.

The table was cold, hard, and clinical, nothing inviting about it. The paper sheet crinkled as the table moved into the scanner. The robotic instructions prompted, "Breathe. Hold. Your. Breath."

I was holding my breath waiting for a diagnosis and a treatment plan, but I didn't need to. Whatever the result, God and I would face it together. He had implored, "Be still, and know that I am God" (Ps. 46:10).

The scan would hopefully identify any physical abnormality contributing to my pain and discomfort. Yet God already knew my condition, and he knew my heart's attitude. Even modern medicine wasn't that good. "Search me, God, and know my heart; test me and know my anxious thoughts" (Ps. 139:23).

As I hoped for answers from this procedure, my condition took me to my knees in prayer, seeking God, his will for me, and what he wanted me to learn through this experience. I cared more about becoming closer in my relationship with God and stronger in my faith. If God used this experience toward that end, then it served a greater purpose.

The pain, suffering, and possible diagnoses ushered in their fair share of anxious thoughts. I chose to seek God in prayer and the pages of his Word and to capture my anxious thoughts, remembering that God hadn't given me the spirit of fear but of power, love, and a sound mind. I repented for entertaining the spirit of fear and instead chose to accept God's peace.

My circumstances didn't surprise God, nor were they too big for him to handle. The pain constantly signaled there was something offensive and unwanted within my body. More importantly, I didn't want anything offensive and unwanted within my heart that pained my heavenly Father. Through prayer, I sought God's opinion about both my physical and my spiritual condition.

We all experience trials. I admitted to a friend that I didn't particularly want this one. It was painful, unpleasant, and, if I entertained negative thoughts, frightening. If I had to endure, I wanted God to teach me whatever lessons he had for me in and through it. I desired to consider it all joy, for rich fruit grows in the valley (James 1:2–4).

A friend often says, "Doctors diagnose and treat. Surgeons operate. God heals." While I sought doctors to diagnose and treat what ailed me, I sought God to search my physical body and the condition of my heart and to heal anything that violated how he had created them so that I could be fully restored in his sight. He is Jehovah Rapha, the God who heals.

We have the power of the great I AM living within us. He promises that we can do all things through his strength (Phil. 4:13). The key is not who we are but who we are in Christ. He's our courage, strength, and wisdom. He promises that when we seek him and his wisdom, he will give it abundantly (James 1:5). When we seek him, we will find him, and when we find him, we can rest in him.

Power from Standing and Resisting

Sometimes life is just hard, and sometimes the enemy puts up great opposition. As I mentioned, the day my book *Hope Prevails* released, my husband was diagnosed with cancer. That was no coincidence. Then when the companion Bible study released, the enemy waged war again. Honestly, I don't care about the enemy's happiness. I don't serve him. I serve the God of peace and hope, and I answer to him.

Still, the enemy pulled out all the stops to make this journey difficult. So I put a stake in the ground and said, "No more! Not today, enemy! I've had enough." I had been playing Hillsong's song "Not Today" and declared aloud that today was not the enemy's day to mess with me or my family.

When the enemy seeks to make us worried, anxious, or fearful, we can stand and resist the devil. "Resist the devil, and he will flee from you" (James 4:7 KJV). We can fight with Scripture. Consistent with God's truth, we can declare, in Jesus's name, that no weapon formed against us will prevail (Isa. 54:17). And ultimately, we know that the battle is the Lord's. "Do not be afraid or discouraged because of this vast army. For the battle is not yours, but God's" (2 Chron. 20:15).

That's where I landed. I was going to stand on God's Word and on his promises. When the enemy throws his arrows, I don't worry, because God promised to fight for us! "You shall not fear them, for it is the LORD your God who fights for you" (Deut. 3:22 ESV). When we have done everything we know, we can stand and watch God fight for us. With a single rock, David defeated Goliath. We only need faith in the Rock to conquer our giants of worry, anxiety, and fear.

Your Rx

1. Look up the following verses: 2 Chronicles 20:15; Psalm 17:6; and Philippians 4:8–9. Then write them on index cards and place them where you will see them frequently. Read each of these passages aloud three times daily, committing them to memory.

2. Make two columns on a sheet of paper or in a journal. As you become aware of your anxieties, log those anxious thoughts on one side. On the other side, write God's promises that refute those thoughts. Each time you are worried or afraid, read through them, reciting the promises aloud.

3. Of the ways discussed in this chapter that we receive power, which area do you need to grow in? Pray and ask God for his help.

My Prayer for You

Heavenly Father, we know that you do not give us the spirit of fear but instead power, love, and a sound mind. I pray for the one reading these words right now that you would minister to their anxious heart and replace all worry, anxiety, and fear with your peace and calm assurance. Remind them of your truth, which is greater than anything they might come up against. Rebuke the spirit of fear and in its place loose your peace to every cell of their being. Thank you, Lord, that you are Shalom, our perfect peace. In Jesus's name, amen.

Recommended Playlist

"Stand in Your Love," Gateway Music, © 2018 by Gateway Music

"Real Love," Hillsong, © 2016 by Hillsong Church T/A Hillsong Music Australia

"Living Water," Gateway Music, © 2018 by Gateway Music

"Greater Is He," Blanca, © 2015 by Word Records

"Here in the Presence," Elevation Worship, © 2017 by Elevation Church

"Only King Forever," 7eventh Time Down, © 2017 by BEC Recordings

"Resurrection Power," Chris Tomlin, © 2018 by Sparrow (SPR)

10

Live in His Perfect Love

As the Father has loved me, so have I loved you. Now remain in my love.

John 15:9

The shape of true love isn't a diamond. It's a cross.

Alicia Bruxvoort

In the last chapter, we discussed our first weapon in the battle against worry, anxiety, and fear: reclaiming God's power in us. Christ's unconditional, everlasting, and perfect love is the second of our three primary weapons. Someone who died to rescue us loves us more than we will ever know or appreciate. Christ's ultimate display of love by dying on the cross put an end to Satan's ability to defeat us, but we must choose to receive and live in his love.

Up until Jesus's death and resurrection, people's faith was based on their belief in what *would come* and what *would ultimately be*. They believed what was foretold. That, to me, takes great faith. But because Jesus came, we can put our faith in the One who is who he says he is and who did what he said he would do. We have the advantage of remembering history and using God's faithfulness to buoy our faith.

When Jesus uttered, "It is finished" from the cross (John 19:30), he put an end to any reason for worry, anxiety, and fear. But on resurrection Sunday, Jesus proved that he is truly greater than the enemy of our souls (1 John 4:4). I believe that if we asked Jesus about the things that tempt us to worry, be anxious, and fear, he would simply answer, "It is finished."

Jesus said that we can possess his peace because he overcame the world when he declared, "It is finished." "I have told you these things, so that in me you may have peace. In this world you will have trouble. But take heart! I have overcome the world" (John 16:33). A friend of mine frequently reminds me, "The enemy may have power, but he has no authority because of Jesus's sacrifice."

When we're tempted to worry, we can instead trust the finished work of the cross and the One who overcame the world so that we can experience peace. If he could defeat death, he can manage whatever concerns us.

Receive His Love through Praise and Worship

Years ago, during a bout of prolonged and severe illness, nothing clarified how much God loved me like saturating myself in praise and worship music. Even when I was unable to praise God with my mouth, I could sing from my heart. David was a master of praise. Numerous times in the Psalms he declared both his love for God and his praise. My favorite is Psalm 63:3: "Because your love is better than life, my lips will glorify you."

Praise and worship are crucial to maintaining peace. Francis Chan said, "When I am consumed by my problems—stressed out about my life, my family, and my job—I actually convey the belief that I think the circumstances are more important than God's command to always rejoice. In other words, that I have a 'right' to disobey God because of the magnitude of my responsibilities."[1]

Patty shared:

> Fear and anxiety caused me to shut down, isolate, withdraw, and despair. I felt alone, like no one cared. I never thought to turn to God or share my experience with anyone else; others came to me with their problems. Through his Word and teaching, with significant time in his presence, I no longer suffer like before. Now I spot the return of fear and anxiety quickly. Worship is key, along with declaring his truth.

Live in His Love through Remembering

Nothing will disrupt our peace faster than taking our eyes off God and not trusting him to care for us while instead trying to plan, manipulate, and control our circumstances ourselves. God has displayed his love, goodness, and faithfulness toward me, yet when the next mountain obscures my path, it's easy to forget what God has done and believe the facts of the situation instead of the truth that God is, has always been, and will always be faithful to love and care for me. The crux of worry, anxiety, and fear is our lack of trust and our desire to control what happens to us, through us, and around us. Sometimes we need a reminder of God's loving faithfulness to continue trusting him and to stop trying to control the outcome ourselves and instead rest in his peace.

Nothing will disrupt our peace faster than taking our eyes off God.

People like to play "Remember when . . ." when they gather with old friends or family. One of our family favorites is the story of my husband's breakfast on a Saturday morning for our preadolescent boys. As he laid the cinnamon-sugar toast on the table, their eyes got big with the anticipation of a favorite. They each grabbed a slice, took a big bite, then spewed it across the table in disgust and alarm. "Dad, what happened to this? What did you do?" My husband urged them to keep eating, offering that nothing was different from the previous time he had made it. A second bite from each child resulted in more gargoyle faces. A quick check brought my husband to the realization that instead of grabbing the container of homemade cinnamon-sugar, he had grabbed the container of homemade BBQ rub. Yuck! These "Remember when . . ." moments bond us as a family and help us remember the past.

We can use other "Remember when . . ." moments as a defense in our struggle against worry, anxiety, and fear. God instructed his people to construct altars to worship him and to remind them of God's faithfulness to them. Abraham built altars at Shechem and east of Bethel (Gen. 12). His altars reminded him how God provided for, protected, and loved him. Similarly, God had the Hebrews lift large stones from the Jordan riverbed to create an altar memorializing their entry into the promised land by way of a miraculously dry path through the river (Josh. 4).

We can build altars of remembrance as a worshipful reminder of God's faithfulness so that the next time trouble comes and we are tempted to worry or fear, we will be reminded of God's past provision. Such an altar could be a journal of our experiences of answered prayer. Another idea is a photo album of places and situations where God stepped in and intervened. We might record ourselves telling stories of God's supernatural hand on our lives. None of these need be for public consumption or even necessarily for sharing with others. They can serve as personal markers of God's faithfulness to us to help us live in his love.

God's Love Is the Answer

It's no surprise that while writing a book on trading our worries for God's peace, I would experience frequent opportunities to practice what I teach. If not for the frustration, aggravation, and consternation, this might have been comical. But alas, I'm still growing in spiritual maturity.

I traveled to Florida to visit our college-age son and spend time writing. I had just dropped him off at campus and gotten myself settled into a friend's garage apartment when my husband called.

"Pray for me," he started.

"Sure, hon. What's up?"

He shared an issue regarding his health status that had risen to the level of concern in his mind. He wanted to trust his doctor to do the best for him, but he acknowledged not only a physical but also a cognitive and spiritual battle. My husband is normally the least worried, anxious, and fearful individual I know, so when he expresses "concerns," I fight against the temptation to worry.

He also shared that his car didn't want to start that morning and needed a mechanic's assessment. These things never happen at a convenient time.

After hanging up, I returned to my notes and my writing plans for the day only to be interrupted a couple hours later.

"Do you have a minute?" my husband asked, then proceeded without waiting for my answer. "They ripped up the old flooring . . ."

"That's great."

"Yes, but they can't lay the new tile today like we expected. Some repairs need to be made. It'll take a few months."

"Are you kidding me?" was all I could say. We had specifically planned this project while I traveled so I wouldn't be interrupted by the mess or the noise.

"I'm sorry, hon. I've contacted contractors about repairs, but you'll come home to bare concrete throughout the house."

I immediately considered the unanticipated expense, mess, and hassle. If we'd known this previously, we wouldn't have undertaken the project. Now we needed to decide how to handle the three scenarios that had burst on the scene like day-old bubble gum.

Immediately after I hung up with my husband, a friend texted, "How's the writing going?"

I shared our triple whammy issues at home, my veins coursing with frustration. Then I paused. "But I have a choice. I can worry and become anxious and fearful, or I can choose to remember God loves me, he allowed these things to happen, and he will see us through them, so I can keep my peace. This, too, shall pass. We don't prefer any of these situations, *but* I choose to maintain an attitude of gratitude: I'm grateful we have multiple vehicles when one is nonfunctional. I'm grateful his doctor is cautious. I'm grateful we have a home and we could afford new tile. I'm grateful I share the good and hard times with my husband."

I returned to my trip's purpose and refocused my writing efforts, determined to address the problems at home once I returned, but not before. The next afternoon, however, I had yet another opportunity to practice trading my worry, anxiety, and fear for God's perfect peace.

"Unbelievable. *Another* school shooting. How do we keep our children safe?" came a friend's text. "Reports suggest he was mentally ill. What do you think?"

"I've been unplugged . . . don't know anything about it. Where?"

"Parkland, Florida. At least seventeen dead. The suspect is in custody."

Parkland. That sounded familiar. Parkland? We used to live near there. Parkland! I realized why it rang a bell. "Wait! I think that's where my nieces attend school!"

I immediately attempted to contact my brother and nieces, albeit unsuccessfully. I whispered prayers for their safety and for the students and teachers affected while I left messages for family. Moments crawled by like summer slugs until I received word. One of my nieces attended the affected high school. She was physically safe, but she and her peers had suffered a traumatic event no child should endure.

Social media and news outlets were quick to bring up politics, gun control, and mental health. Make no mistake—this tragedy was an evil act in the south Florida community. The enemy came to steal, kill, and destroy within those families, that school, and that community.

This event hit home for me, not just because of my niece's jeopardy but because I had worked as a responder with my fellow interns in conjunction with the Red Cross following the Oklahoma City bombing in 1995. I still can't forget the sights, sounds, and smells of that evil act.

The next day another friend texted, "I couldn't breathe when I saw that shooting. I can't stomach it anymore. I'm honestly battling much anxiety over the state of our world."

Such unwanted situations present us with an opportunity: either give in to the enemy's temptation to worry, be anxious, and fear or stay grounded in the truth that perfect love casts out all fear and allows us to maintain our peace. Love may not be the popular answer, but it is truth. Jesus died on the cross *for* those who committed evil against him *because* he loved. Jesus warned us that trials would come, and we don't have to like them, but God doesn't cause these crises. Jesus also told us that he had overcome it all. In his love for us, he took the sin and evil of this world on him so that we could have a relationship with our heavenly Father and live in his peace. While God doesn't cause these trials, he does lovingly walk hand in hand with us through them (Isa. 43:2–3). My faith remains in God's perfect love, not in the world. That is how we maintain our peace.

Accepting His Love

"If I'm not mistaken, I think I hear the wind crying."

He caught me. My husband and I were walking together on the beach, except he was with me only via cell phone. Through the line, above the roar of the wind and the waves, he heard me crying.

Three times in three days, conversations tugged at my heart and released the valve to my tears, each time catching me off guard. I hadn't felt sad, but I had gone to the beach, my peaceful place, in search of answers from God. Life had taken a fast, unexpected curve, tossing me back and forth with uncertainty, and I needed God's direction.

After hanging up with my husband, I continued walking on the beach, talking to God.

God beckoned me to trust him more. But I protested.

I trusted him to faithfully answer my prayers for the many I regularly prayed for. "That's good," he acknowledged.

I trusted him to answer others' prayers for me. "Mm-hmm," he replied. "And?" I heard in my heart.

"And what?" I retorted to the Lord.

"Do you trust me to answer your prayers for yourself? In fact, do you trust me enough to ask for what's on your heart? Do you trust my love for you enough to believe I will fulfill my promises to you? I've promised in my Word that I will do *more* than anything you could dare to ask or imagine. I'm still waiting for you to ask."

He got me. He knew my heart, and he wanted me to see it also.

In turbulent times, if we do not guard our thoughts, we fall prey to the enemy, who tries to convince us his lies are true. I fell for them, and with them came doubts and questions.

Faced with a significant life change, I questioned everything. How had I gotten here? Should I have seen it coming? Could I have prevented it? Did it reflect God's displeasure with me? Had I misunderstood his purpose, plan, and call for my life? Was I just a slow learner? I felt like I was stranded on an island with only an occasional passerby throwing out a life preserver too flimsy to carry the weight of my burdens. From every direction, I heard God beckon, "Trust me. Don't look to the left or to the right. Don't look behind or ahead. Look up to me and trust. Trust that I love you enough to care for your needs."

I tearfully whispered, "What does that look like, Lord? That's another intangible." (God and I frequently converse about the intangibles like faith, joy, peace, rest, trust, and, yes, love). "How do I do that? Please help my unbelief."

When life hurts, or falls apart, we need to accept his love and remember that, regardless of what our earthly father was like, God is a good Father who loves his children and wants the best for them. We can run to him and find refuge in his loving arms. We don't go through struggles alone. He goes before us. He never leaves us. We are not alone. His continual presence is proof of his love. There is nothing we can do to earn it or to make ourselves worthy of it, but we do choose whether or not to accept it. Accepting God's love is a key step in trusting him. It's hard to trust someone if we don't believe they love us and care about us.

I recalled two Scripture passages: "But seek first His kingdom and His righteousness, and all these things will be added to you" (Matt. 6:33 NASB) and "You will seek me and find me when you seek me with all your heart" (Jer. 29:13). I sought him, and his love held me secure under the safe shadow of his wing (Ps. 91:1). We can't live in God's perfect love until we accept that he loves us. Accepting God's love requires our trust.

Here is Nancy's experience of God's transforming love:

> Fear and anxiety began after I succumbed to a cult. I dove into a confused state, disconnecting from loved ones and my purpose for living. Every decision, every choice kept me stuck, immobilized by fear, believing any move I made was wrong and would condemn me. Trapped by terror, I only wanted to escape my mind. I desired to stop thinking and feeling. This included the option of dying. My soul and spirit were trapped in what felt like the terrors of hell.
>
> Decades later, I possess an extreme belief and sense of God's unconditional love for me. My faith in my loving Creator has been restored. I realize what God has done for me through the miracle of his Son, Jesus. Believing and accepting that I am his child restored and sustained my life's purpose. Realizing his forgiveness, I am no longer stuck and unable to make choices, no longer immobilized by fear and anxiety. Knowing his unconditional love for me prevents the extreme darkness, confusion, and terrors that previously defined my very existence.

In Case You Wondered If God Loves You

Friend, I feel your heartache and I know your pain. As your tears flow and you feel alone, know that God promised never to leave you

(Heb. 13:5). When you look around and wish you were more like "them," remember that God delights in *you* (Zeph. 3:17). When you feel stressed and overwhelmed, take comfort in knowing that God has promised that because he began a good work in you, he will see it through to the end. He won't give up on you (Phil. 1:6). When you feel like a failure or you are not measuring up, don't give up. You can do anything with God's help (Phil. 4:13).

The truth is, those thoughts and feelings you have (that you are alone, aren't good enough, can't handle the stress, are a failure, etc.) are lies—lies from the enemy, who desires to steal, kill, and destroy anything that would help you experience the peace, joy, and abundant life God desires for us (John 10:10).

I encourage you to memorize the verses I cited above so that the next time the enemy whispers lies to you, you can proclaim God's truth. The enemy won't back down until you are convinced!

God loves you when:

- you feel lonely
- you are stressed
- you feel inadequate
- you fail
- life is uncertain
- you feel weary or angry
- you are worried, afraid, or anxious

God loves you because he *is* love. He can't *not* love you. He promises that nothing (not your sin, your failures, your feelings, your circumstances) can come between you and his love. You can't stop him from loving you. He isn't an angry God out to punish you but a merciful God seeking to express his love to you in innumerable ways.

The world is evil, ridiculing, and unpredictable. We experience this frequently, perhaps constantly. This makes it difficult to see God as other than capricious and condemning. But God is not like the world. The world will never exemplify God's love; it can't. To fully appreciate God's love for us, we must know his character. God is merciful, loving, and constant. His love is perfect and complete. But to know God's character, we have to see him as he is. To see him, we have to have a relationship with him. Can you see him? Do you know him? Will you accept his gift of love today?

God's Love Is Good

It doesn't matter what is going on in our lives, whether good, bad, or uncertain. God's love is good. Not only that, but because he loves us, God promises to work *all* things together for our good. Do you believe that?

I wondered about that today. Even while writing this chapter, painful circumstances and brokenness seemed never-ending—within myself, my family, my friends.

Frequently, the enemy works to trap me in a cycle of worrying.

What if the chemotherapy doesn't work and my husband dies from the cancer?

What if I don't find suitable replacement staff and I'm forced to close my private practice? How will we pay the mortgage? Health insurance? College tuition?

What if this physical pain never relents and I never find relief? What if it becomes disabling?

What if my words of wisdom and advice don't help or offer comfort? What then? Am I useless or a failure?

None of my adverse circumstances or any of your painful trials negates the fact that God's love is good. None. We must hold on to that. He warned trials would come, but remember, because he loves us, he overcame them all.

Jesus discussed peace before warning of life's difficulties. He explained that we don't have to sacrifice our peace when trouble befalls us. In John 16:33, Jesus basically declared, "I've made a way for you to rest peacefully regardless of what difficulties threaten you." Trials, difficulties, and pain will come, but our Advocate, our Savior, promised that he overcame them all. Therefore, we can experience peace *through* them. If we could see the end from the beginning, we would see that just as God has lovingly promised, he works all things together to benefit us because he loves us.

Jesus's expression of love on the cross removed all of anxiety's power.

This doesn't mean there won't be pain. I wish it weren't so. I'm sure Jesus did too. He felt our pain as they pushed a crown of thorns upon his forehead. As they beat his back and face until he was unrecognizable. As he carried his weighty cross up that grueling hill. As they drove spikes in his hands and feet. But Jesus endured the torture so that eventually we would experience the ultimate good because of his love-fueled suffering. Jesus's expression of love on the cross removed all of anxiety's power. Anxiety has no authority to rule our lives unless we allow it.

God's Love Is Trustworthy

"Trust me. I promise I'll go easy on you if you're nice to me," implored my young son.

As a family, we enjoy playing games together, especially cards. This particular game required that we exchange three of our cards with each other . . . a risky endeavor. You never know if what you will receive will be worse than the medicine you dish out. I agreed with my son's pleas to be kind only to receive some of the worst cards in the deck in return. He laughed, leaving me aghast.

Unfortunately for him, that little childhood maneuver meant that in successive games I would not trust him again, for he had shown himself untrustworthy. A valuable lesson, and one we've repeatedly referenced to help teach him about trustworthy friends, acquaintances, and even teachers. This included teaching him that those who really love us are going to be trustworthy, whereas those who only say they love us will usually have their own well-being as their priority.

God also continues to woo me into a deeper trust walk with him. It's often been more like an ungraceful balance beam maneuver—with me falling off and trying again—than a beautiful ballet. He knows my heart, and he knows my wounds. He knows in whom I mistakenly placed my trust only to get hurt . . . and he hurt for me. If only I had kept my eyes solely on him, he might have saved me from that wounding, although sometimes we get so focused on ourselves that we forget that the storms may have a greater purpose in our lives. Yet because God loves me, I can trust him to protect me.

God knows my longing to go deeper with him; he knows my hesitancy and my fear. He knows it would be beautiful if I trusted him more fully, in turn knowing him more deeply. He also knows my reluctance. Trusting God more requires that I show him more of me, the parts I don't let anyone see, the parts that grieve me to see. When others find out about our faults and past mistakes, they may react with rejection and abandonment. But God loves us so much, with such a protective love, that he will never reject or abandon us. He doesn't want anything to interfere with our relationship with him. "Those who know your name trust in you, for you, LORD, have never forsaken those who seek you" (Ps. 9:10). Because God loves us, we can trust him to protect us.

> *When self-protection is our goal, there's no room for trusting God's protective love.*

Fear is the opposite of trust. When self-protection is our goal, there's no room for trusting God's protective love. That self-protective stance leaves us lonely and unwilling to invite others in, including God. Fear is not from God. It is a direct attack from the one who wants to prevent us from drawing close to God or knowing his trustworthy love.

In reality, we are powerless to protect ourselves. Fear doesn't protect. So self-protection is futile. What we really need is a sure protector—and only a trustworthy God can be that for us. That's a pretty convincing argument to demolish the self-protective walls, receive his love, and trust him. The more we try to be our own provider and protector, the less we experience God's blessings because we limit him. If we trust in his provision and his timing, we open the door to his abundant blessing, provision, and protection. "But I trust in your unfailing love; my heart rejoices in your salvation" (Ps. 13:5). Where do you need to relinquish self-protection and let God protect you?

God's Love Drives Out Fear

Scripture declares, "Such love has no fear, because perfect love expels all fear. If we are afraid, it is for fear of punishment, and this shows that we have not fully experienced his perfect love" (1 John 4:18 NLT). When we fully appreciate the extent of God's perfect love for us, we can trust him and not give in to fear. We can rest in the security that our Father protects, provides, strengthens, supports, forgives, and goes to battle for us.

Will I trust the Lord even if I lose my husband? My children? My friends? If I no longer have my business? My dream? Will I trust unswervingly despite my circumstances?

Scripture tells us that those who trust in the Lord will not be put to shame (Rom. 10:11). When difficulties come, we often ask why. Yet knowing why rarely brings peace. Peace comes from trusting God, focusing on him, despite not knowing why. "You will keep in perfect peace all who trust in you, all whose thoughts are fixed on you!" (Isa. 26:3 NLT). Furthermore, he promises to help us and shield us if we trust in him. "You who fear him, trust in the LORD—he is their help and shield" (Ps. 115:11).

A recent situation tried my faith and resulted in frustration and pain. I prayed about it for months. God showed me a picture of the situation, and I believed the outcome would align with what he had shown me. The circumstances required that I take a stand for myself and my beliefs and what I believed God intended. I had to step outside my comfort zone, step into bold courage, and stand up for the conviction God had placed in my heart.

Things didn't happen the way I believed they would, nor in accordance with the picture he had given me. I brought this to God's attention (as if he wasn't already aware). "God, I don't understand. Why would you give me this picture if the outcome isn't matching up?" I prayed that three consecutive days until I let him speak to my heart.

"Do you trust me and my love for you?" he asked. He meant, "Do you trust me even when you don't know why?"

"Yes, Lord. I still don't understand why you would show me this image when the reality doesn't match. But I don't need to understand. I choose to trust you anyway."

When we can say, "Yes, Lord, I trust you. You are love. I was created by you to love you and to be loved by you. You are my provider, my Savior, my protector. I trust you in all these areas," then we can walk without fear. Perfect love drives out fear, and peace rules. In trusting him and trusting that he does everything out of love for us, we will not be disappointed. We demonstrate real faith when our circumstances tell us we should be hopeless and afraid, yet we rest in God's love anyway. That is when we fully live in the covering of his love, and peace prevails.

Your Rx

1. Look up the following verses: Psalm 13:5; 63:3; Isaiah 26:3; Romans 10:11; and 1 John 4:18. Then write them on index cards and place them where you will see them frequently. Read each of these passages aloud three times daily, committing them to memory.

2. Ask God what kind of worshipful altar of remembrance he wants you to build. Begin that today.

3. Write a letter to God reflecting to him all the ways he displays his love to you. Ask him to show you new and deeper ways. Express your gratitude and love to him in return.

My Prayer for You

Father, thank you that because of your perfect love for us, it is finished, and Satan's power to torment is over. Thank you for overcoming the world. We choose to receive your power and your peace, to walk in your victory, to have your mind, to walk in one accord. We choose our words wisely to align with your truth, to trust you and not the enemy. We choose to trade our worry, anxiety, and fear for your power, love, and sound mind. In Jesus's name, amen.

Recommended Playlist

"Deliverance," Gateway Music, © 2018 by Gateway Music

"One Thing Remains," Bethel Music and Brian Johnson, © 2014 by Bethel Music

"Love Came Down," Brian Johnson, © 2015 by Integrity Music

"Build My Life," Housefires, ℗© 2016 by Housefires

"Old for New," Hannah McClure, Bethel Music, ℗© 2017 by Bethel Music

"Your Love Defends Me," Matt Maher, ℗ 2017 by Provident Label Group LLC

11

Use Your Sound Mind

They are confident and fearless
and can face their foes triumphantly.

Psalm 112:8 NLT

The greatest weapon against stress is our ability to choose one
thought over another.

William James

God gives us his power through the shed blood of his Son on the cross, our first weapon in the battle against worry, anxiety, and fear, and his perfect love to cast out all fear, our second weapon. He also gives us a third weapon in our arsenal against worry, anxiety, and fear: a sound mind, which we received when he bestowed on us the mind of Christ. "'Who has known the mind of the Lord so as to instruct him?' But we have the mind of Christ" (1 Cor. 2:16).

What a gift to know that when the enemy comes knocking, selling his lies, we aren't obligated to open the door. Instead, we can rely on the mind of Christ, which never steers us wrong but instead gives life and peace to our souls. "The mind governed by the flesh is death, but the mind governed by the Spirit is life and peace" (Rom. 8:6).

Having the mind of Christ means we depend on him to lead, doing as he asks and not relying on ourselves. Doesn't that take a weight off your shoulders? Jesus perfectly modeled a life devoted to pleasing his Father. "By myself I can do nothing . . . for I seek not to please myself but him who sent me" (John 5:30). In seeking to know God's will and way for our lives, we just need to look at Jesus's example. "Whoever has seen me has seen the Father. . . . I am in the Father and the Father is in me" (John 14:9, 11 ESV).

> *As we learn to replace those lies with thoughts that agree with God, we exchange worry, anxiety, and fear for his perfect peace.*

The enemy desperately wants us to believe his lies. As we learn to replace those lies with thoughts that agree with God, we exchange worry, anxiety, and fear for his perfect peace. "Do not be conformed to this world, but be transformed by the renewal of your mind, that by testing you may discern what is the will of God, what is good and acceptable and perfect" (Rom. 12:2 ESV).

Choose Your Focus

A professor distributed a surprise test facedown on each student's desk. Once each student possessed the test, the professor instructed the students to turn the paper over and write an essay regarding what they saw on the paper: a single small black dot in the middle of the white piece of paper.

The students glanced down at the page, then up at the professor, then at one another with unspoken questions in their expressions. The teacher offered no further explanation before sitting down at her desk. Each student began writing.

After the allotted time, the professor collected all the tests. Much to the students' surprise, she read their essays aloud to the class. When she exhausted the pile of essays, the professor explained that she would not grade the exam, but she hoped each student would learn from the experience.

Each student focused on some aspect of the black dot. They had written about the size of the dot, the color, the diameter, and the way the dot blemished the otherwise clean white page. Not a single student focused on the white space surrounding the dot, which encompassed much more space than the conspicuous smudge. She further explained that so often this exemplifies our tendency in life: we focus on the few things that go wrong, are negative, or bother us rather than the many good, positive things we could choose to make our focus.

Since hearing that story, I have challenged myself to intentionally shift my focus to the positive aspects of situations. Otherwise, negativity can overwhelm and override my focus and my attitude, resulting in a cascade effect: I become negative and feel defeated about other, unrelated situations as well. Philippians 4:8–9 encourages, "Fix your thoughts on what is true, and honorable, and right, and pure, and lovely, and admirable. Think about things that are excellent and worthy of praise. Keep putting into practice all you learned and received from me—everything you heard from me and saw me doing. Then the God of peace will be with you" (NLT).

A direct correlation exists between our thought lives and the degree to which we experience God's presence and his peace. This passage teaches that if we keep our thoughts on the positive things from him, things worthy of praise, *then* we will experience peace. Rather than focusing on the negative black dot of our circumstances, which ushers in worry, anxiety, and fear, let's pay more attention to the beautiful, praiseworthy white space of his trustworthy promises and truths.

I have heard it said that "your faith can move mountains and your doubt can create them."[1] The wrong focus contributes to doubt, robbing us of peace. Focusing on Jesus lends us faith and courage to face, with peace, the trials we struggle to humanly understand.

Here is Alison's experience:

> My husband and I face more than the typical parenthood
> stresses: our three children all have disabilities. As they
> grew, my anxiety increased. Scary statistics and their non-
> typical imperfections have been challenging. After many
> hours of crying my fears, my hurts, and my ongoing worries
> out to God, even thinking it was my fault, God showed me
> how he sees our situation. "Jesus answered, 'It was not that
> this man sinned, or his parents, but that the works of God
> might be displayed in him'" (John 9:3 ESV).
>
> His plan for us as parents has been to totally trust him.
> He reminded me of 2 Corinthians 4:18: "So we fix our eyes
> not on what is seen, but on what is unseen, since what is
> seen is temporary, but what is unseen is eternal" (NIV). We
> must focus on God rather than our problems. For years, I
> suffered in silence from depression and anxiety, but shifting
> my focus was key to my healing and recovery. The wisdom,
> love, and truth in the pages of God's Word may not change
> your earthly situation, but I guarantee they will change your
> heart, your perspective, and your life.

Separate Facts from Truth

Have you experienced discouragement due to the facts surrounding
your circumstances? Have you ever been paralyzed by fear stemming
from a seemingly devastating situation?

I have.

As I already mentioned, when I was fifteen, my father passed away
unexpectedly from a heart attack. My first thought that awful night
was, *How will I help my family make ends meet?* I feared for our survival. My father had supported us. My mother was from another country and had no education or employable skill. I plotted and planned
to increase my babysitting, lawn mowing, and house cleaning until I
could secure full-time employment.

For decades after my father's death, I allowed fear to maintain a scarcity mind-set. I falsely believed, "If it is to be, it is up to me." I believed that God could have prevented my father's death; since he didn't, how could I trust him to care for my family and provide all we needed? So I took it upon myself to provide, a role God never intended for me to assume.

Remember our discussion of the widow of Zarephath in chapter 7? Having experienced lean times, the pain of loss, and devastating life circumstances, I can relate to her. Can't you imagine her anguish over her lean conditions and the desperation in her heart knowing that she and her son were one meal away from death? How frustrating, irritating, and aggravating when a stranger asked her for something she intended to give her own child, as if he was oblivious to her lack. Still, she gave to Elijah, and God faithfully provided more oil and flour to refill her jars.

Despite God's miraculous, faithful provision, she became wracked with anxiety when her son died. Her faith plummeted, and she blamed Elijah. "What do you have against me, man of God? Did you come to remind me of my sin and kill my son?" (1 Kings 17:18). Even Elijah seemingly acquiesced to worry and fear as he begged God to save her son.

Have you ever forgotten God's faithfulness when you encountered difficulty? When facts are compelling, sometimes our faith wavers. The facts may suggest more month than paycheck, cancer's presence, an unfaithful spouse, a distressed family member, or other challenge. But the truth remains: God is faithful, he promises to supply all our needs, and he declared that his plans for us are good and include a hope-filled future. Sometimes we must undervalue the facts and place our faith in the truth.

Talk Back to Anxiety

One of the most important lessons I learned through my journey out of depression and anxiety was the importance of paying attention to our thoughts and words and taking each thought captive rather than mindlessly accepting the enemy's lies, which leads us into worry, anxiety, and fear. "We destroy arguments and every lofty opinion raised against the knowledge of God, and take every thought captive to obey Christ" (2 Cor. 10:5 ESV).

Karen shared her experience:

> When my son served in the military in Iraq, he went to sleep many nights to the sound of gunfire and had to wear full battle gear just to walk from one building to another. I took my thoughts captive, did not dwell on what could happen, and prayed and praised the Lord for surrounding him and caring for him.

"I heard your voice in my head this morning," my friend said on the telephone.

"I hope that was good!"

"It was. My heart felt like it was beating out of my chest. I feared I was having a heart attack. But I knew with the recent stress it was anxiety."

"When did you hear my voice?"

"I heard you say, 'Refuse to fear. God's got this and you. Tell that anxiety to go away.'"

"And?"

"I did. My heart rate returned to normal!"

I chuckled. "I'm not sure if you heard me or the Holy Spirit. Regardless, I'm glad you listened and it helped. Fear and anxiety are destructive liars and have no place in your life. You have power over them, as you proved."

After hanging up, I thought of the years I accepted worry, anxiety, and fear as unwelcome tagalong passengers in the backseat of my life, as if I had no say in the matter. I drove to work daily with a boulder in my stomach and tears streaming down my face. Every morning dread consumed me as my eyes opened. Body aches attested to carrying the weight of the world that was never mine to shoulder.

Then God revealed the truth of 2 Timothy 1:7. I started saying no to that fear. I took back my power and spoke out against its influence, telling it instead that I had the mind of Christ and the same power that raised Christ from the dead (Rom. 8:11).

The enemy tries to paralyze us with fear, when God tells us to pray instead of worry (Phil. 4:6–7). Rather than tolerating its existence, we need to talk back to anxiety and put it in its proper place. Scripture says, "Anxiety weighs down the heart, but a kind word cheers it up" (Prov. 12:25). Sometimes we need to speak that encouraging word to ourselves or receive it by seeking wise counsel, such as from doctors, therapists, or pastors.

> *When you battle worry, anxiety, or fear, talk back to it! Declare it has no useful place in your life, you won't receive it, and it must go, in Jesus's name.*

Jesus essentially told Satan not to hinder him and that Satan was an offense to him (Matt. 16:23). That's how we must view worry, anxiety, and fear as well: a stumbling block put in our path by the enemy intended to make us take our eyes off God, our ultimate provider. Anxiety distracts and dissuades. But if we stay focused on God, he will smooth our path.

Just as Jesus told Satan to leave, and my friend did when encumbered with anxiety, we should do the same with worry, anxiety, and fear. When you battle worry, anxiety, or fear, talk back to it! Declare it has no useful place in your life, you won't receive it, and it must go, in Jesus's name. Then thank God that he promises his perfect peace when you focus on him. "You will keep in perfect peace all who trust in you, all whose thoughts are fixed on you!" (Isa. 26:3 NLT).

Lucretia shared:

> Several years ago, my health declined with atrial fibrillation. I decided that since God didn't give it to me, I wasn't going to agree with it. When I learned that the root cause of AFib is fear/stress/anxiety, I used my God-given authority. After confessing that I had agreed with fear—because it was

physically expressing in my body—I told fear to leave. My symptoms are gone.

Sue shared her experience:

I fell into intense anxiety years ago when, over the course of six weeks, we were forced to move, were betrayed by close family members, causing us to lose a six-figure investment, lost a job, found out my daughter had cancer, and were sued for an unrelated matter. I'd been a Christian for twenty-five years, but nothing prepared me for the repeated battles. I lost everything but my marriage in less than two months: my job, my role as a caretaker, the home where we raised our kids, our retirement investment, and a relationship I had trusted implicitly. Unrelenting anxiety ensued.

After several weeks of major challenges, the night before we were scheduled to move, the anxiety climaxed. My entire body shook, and I had no clue what was happening. Waves of uncontrollable tremors ravaged my whole body, accompanied by desperation. I feared I would die. There was no way to control it. No way to talk myself down. Panic invaded my mind and left an empty, sickening dread. My mind screamed, "No! I cannot move!" but I couldn't do anything about it.

Daily anxiety took over like a relative who moved in uninvited. I suffered constant dread. I constantly felt on edge, always awaiting the next catastrophe. Everything seemed threatening. Leaving the house became increasingly intimidating because every nerve was on high alert expecting bad things to happen. I worried I was losing my mind because the confident, capable, optimistic person I had always been could not be found.

The answer was Christ—humble submission to his will and plan. My biggest breakthrough came when I adopted Jesus's unwavering faith in his Father and finally said, "God, I accept what has happened. I trust you will use it for my good and your glory." That moment of acceptance was revolutionary for relinquishing control and self-will in favor of trusting God's perfect plan. I trusted him, not my feelings.

My only hope was God. I spent hours alone in prayer, worship, and Scripture reading. It wasn't a quick road back, but I no longer suffer from anxiety. When it wells up, I reject it. God won those battles for me. I don't even fight them. I don't question anxiety. I don't try to manage it or cope with it. I refuse it. Period. I know the truth: I am not an anxious person; I am God's beloved child. Anxiety and worry have no place in my life. I know God doesn't intend for his children to live in anxiety. My confidence is in God's promises. He says, "Be anxious for nothing."

Change Your Thoughts

Worry, anxiety, and fear can't be permitted to rule our lives. "The mind governed by the Spirit is life and peace" (Rom. 8:6). It's difficult to effectively fight a battle until we know our opponent. We must identify the existence and working of the enemy, particularly through the spirit of fear in our lives. After we recognize the enemy's influence in our lives, we must repent for agreeing with him, then request and receive God's forgiveness. It's imperative that we rebuke him and renounce his presence in Jesus's name. When we submit to God and resist the devil, God's peace (which defies our comprehension) prevails. In our union with Jesus's resurrection, he gave open access to perfect peace. We experience this peaceful existence by persistently focusing our thoughts on Christ and turning away from our natural tendency to worry. When our thoughts stray from his peace, we must recognize the enemy's temptation, repent, and receive God's gracious forgiveness.

Ecklund shared her experience:

I was diagnosed with depression and anxiety while in college. I didn't want to accept the diagnosis or the need for medicine and counseling. I entered into nearly three years of counseling with a Christian psychologist and a psychiatrist. My pastor provided wise counsel, explaining that there are thirty-one proverbs, one for each day of the month, and if you read one proverb and five psalms each day, you will read through both books each month. I still revert to this formula when facing valleys. Over twenty-five years later, I have systems in place to help me, but it is because of Jesus Christ that I am alive today. Tie a knot on the end of the rope and hold on to Jesus. He will never leave you nor forsake you. He is there in the midnight hours when you lack the words to pray and are murmuring and groaning before him. He comforts and gives peace.

Have you ever been stuck in a period of intense trials? Perhaps in your heart you trust that God is good and cares for you, but still . . . you have moments, like before going to bed or in the middle of the night, when your mind runs amok with stressful thoughts, prompting fear. Despite trying, you can't stop the hamster wheel of fearful thoughts from replaying in your mind.

Connie described:

Fear in the pit of my stomach and worry over losing someone I love wake me up. My sister and my husband have health issues. My sister battled cancer for five years; instead of remission, it actually spread. If I allowed the fear to move from the pit of my stomach, I knew it would advance and consume me. I knew if I allowed it to grow, it would overwhelm, overtake, and consume me like a giant monster.

I woke in the middle of the night with fear. I cried out to God for answers and asked how to stop these feelings. He directed me to put my headphones on at night and saturate my mind with truth. I play Christian spiritual teachings at night so that if I wake up, my fearful thoughts don't take control. These words of truth were the first conscious thoughts I had, which helped me resist fear.

We know the command to "fear not," but how? We frequently hear that we must turn our thoughts to the Lord instead of to our fears, but we are seldom given strategies for doing so. God knew we would experience worry, anxiety, and fear, and he included over three hundred Scripture passages encouraging us—no, commanding us— not to fear. God never allows us to experience temptation without also giving us a way to escape it (1 Cor. 10:13), and the same is true for worry, anxiety, and fear.

Nine Ways to Fight Back with a Sound Mind

There are nine basic ways to operate with a sound mind to change our thoughts and to fight against the spirit of fear and regain God's peace.

1. Recognize that worry, anxiety, and fear exist.

We cannot battle what we don't know exists. Hosea 4:6 declares, "My people are destroyed from lack of knowledge." Only when we know a giant exists, can we determine the most effective battle plan.

2. Recognize where worry, anxiety, and fear originate.

Scripture clearly teaches that neither people nor circumstances cause our worry, anxiety, and fear. Remember, they come from the spirit of fear (2 Tim. 1:7). Since the Garden of Eden, humankind has battled an enemy bent on our destruction, while Jesus came to give us a full life (John 10:10). Scripture explains that our battle is with evil forces of darkness. "For our struggle is not against flesh and blood, but against the rulers, against the authorities, against the powers of this dark world and against the spiritual forces of evil in the heavenly realms" (Eph. 6:12).

3. Recognize that negative thoughts are not yours.

The enemy, the father of lies (John 8:44), continuously whispers, "What if?" to tempt us to worry. And as if worry and fear weren't enough, the enemy also loves to torment God's children with guilt and shame. The truth is that we have the mind of Christ and those anxious thoughts are not our own. We must utilize the armor of God to fight against the real enemy.

Emotions are the outward manifestations of the thoughts we believe. So when we feel anxious, it's because we've believed thoughts that prompt anxiety. Instead of acting on our feelings, we must speak out against the thoughts that caused them. We must recognize that the thoughts are from the enemy, refute them, and speak back to them.

> *Emotions are the outward manifestations of the thoughts we believe. So when we feel anxious, it's because we've believed thoughts that prompt anxiety.*

For example, if you feel anxious, say something out loud like, "No! I will not be afraid! God gave me power, love, and a sound mind instead of fear. God cares for me and says to give him all my concerns. Instead of being afraid, I will trust God." If you do this enough, your feelings will align with your words!

4. Ask God what is prompting your worry, anxiety, and fear.

When we recognize the presence of worry, anxiety, or fear, because of physical or emotional symptoms, sometimes we may not readily identify what thoughts or beliefs triggered our anxious response. In such times, we can ask God to reveal our inaccurate thoughts. He delights in shining the light of truth in darkness. "When the Spirit of truth comes, he will guide you into all truth" (John 16:13 NLT).

5. Counter worry, anxiety, and fear with God's truth.

Once we recognize worry, anxiety, and fear for what they are and what led to them, we can refute them with the truth of God's Word. "For the word of God is alive and active. Sharper than any double-edged sword, it penetrates even to dividing soul and spirit, joints and marrow; it judges the thoughts and attitudes of the heart" (Heb. 4:12). When Jesus died, he left the Holy Spirit, who reminds us of truth. But the Holy Spirit can only remind us of truth we know. If we don't know God's Word, he cannot remind us of that truth in difficult circumstances. So we must learn what Scripture says and keep it in the forefront of our minds.

I wrote Scripture passages on Post-it Notes, then placed those notes where I would see them: the bathroom mirror, light switches, my dashboard. Every time I saw one, I read it aloud, washing my mind in the water of the Word, consistent with Ephesians 5:26. I intentionally read Scripture aloud because our faith is strengthened when we hear God's Word (Rom. 10:17). The more I recited it, the more I believed it and it became ingrained in me.

As my needs changed, so did my Scripture focus. Sometimes fear and anxiety overwhelmed, while other times I needed encouragement emphasizing peace or joy. As I memorized verses and no longer needed the visual reminder, I removed the notes and taped them on a poster board for less frequent reference. Eventually, I transferred them to a spiral binder that I carried in my purse.

Connie shared:

> After my mom died, I cried daily for months. I cried out to God to help me and heal my shattered heart, to pause my life so I could heal. God answered that cry by eliminating my job. In that pause, God helped me lay down all of my past, hurt, shame, heartbreak, shattered dreams, broken relationships, and regret. I opened the Bible, and the words jumped off the pages at me! For the first time, I understood them. The Word was alive! God led me to Romans 8:28, where I learned that all my pain has a purpose. I have a purpose! He chose me. I am not garbage. I am fearfully and wonderfully made, highly sought after and desired. On my knees, I gave everything to God, stepped out in faith, trusted his promises, and stayed obediently faithful!

When plagued with worry, anxiety, or fear, remember these Scripture passages: "Don't be afraid, for I am with you. Don't be discouraged, for I am your God. I will strengthen you and help you. I will hold you up with my victorious right hand" (Isa. 41:10 NLT). "This is my command—be strong and courageous! Do not be afraid or discouraged. For the LORD your God is with you wherever you go" (Josh. 1:9 NLT). I have provided a free printable list of additional Scriptures to help you, which you can download at https://drmichellebengtson.com/scriptures-combat-worry-fear-anxiety/. Proclaim those truths aloud every time worry, anxiety, or fear tempts you.

6. Declare your trust in God.

Instead of believing the enemy's lies, we must tell God that we trust him to handle our situation. "When I am afraid, I put my trust in you" (Ps. 56:3). Then we need to thank him ahead of time for his answers. When we entrust our worries into God's care, holding nothing back and thanking him for his provision, we can live from a place of peace (Phil. 4:6–7). You might want to refer to the "Five Keys to Trusting God" in chapter 2.

7. Pray Scripture prayers.

The most beneficial prayers incorporate God's Word. God will never renege on a promise. Praying his Word reminds him of his promises. "It is the same with my word. I send it out, and it always produces fruit. It will accomplish all I want it to, and it will prosper everywhere I send it" (Isa. 55:11 NLT).

Here is Jenni's experience:

> I prayed Scripture over my daughter. I prayed for mercy and grace to wash over her. I asked the Holy Spirit to hover over her and keep her safe. I thanked God in advance for her salvation. I played worship music and let the words wash over

me, resulting in more prayers. When I exhausted words to
pray, I prayed in the Spirit. I did this until peace washed over
me.

You might pray something similar to this:

*Dear God, you know my situation, and you know that my natural
inclination is to worry and to feel anxious and afraid. But you have
not given me the spirit of fear. Instead, you have given me power,
love, and a sound mind. You told me not to be afraid, so it is possible for me to endure these circumstances without fear. You are
my God and have promised to be with me, strengthen me, and
help me, upholding me with your victorious right hand. Instead
of being afraid, I trust you. You will not fail me. Because of you, I
can be strong and courageous. Thank you for going with me. In
Jesus's name, amen.*

8. Tell the enemy to leave.

Jesus modeled the perfect response to Satan's temptations when
he said, "Get away from me, Satan! You are a dangerous trap to me.
You are seeing things merely from a human point of view, not from
God's" (Matt. 16:23 NLT). As we discussed in chapter 9, Jesus has
given us the same power and authority to put the enemy in his place,
with God's help.

In addition to telling the enemy to leave, we must submit to God's
will and his timing and take a stand against the enemy's deception.
When we do, he must leave. "So humble yourselves before God. Resist
the devil, and he will flee from you" (James 4:7 NLT).

Karen shared her experience:

One day I realized I'd been plagued by fear because of the
enemy, and I needed freedom. I shared my history with my
husband. He took my hands and prayed over me, and then
he held me for a long time. I felt free, out in the open, and
my husband covered me as my husband under God and as

my intercessor to pray for me and help me learn to fight the enemy. I discovered that the more I came under the authority of my husband as my spiritual covering, the freer I was to become the woman God created me to be. I lay on the floor facedown with fear in one hand and anxiety in the other and opened my hands to God, releasing both to my heavenly Father in the name of Jesus. From that moment on, I knew I was free. I went through the Scriptures about fear, condemnation, and unforgiveness. I spoke them out loud and received my healing. I learned all I could about who I am in Christ. The Holy Spirit lives within me, and I am no longer afraid! When the enemy tries to bring fear back into my life, as soon as I recognize the symptoms, I rebuke him in Jesus's name. If the enemy is relentless, I ask my husband to pray with me. We pray for each other every morning and evening.

9. Remain alert.

We cannot become complacent but must remain alert to the enemy's influence. "Be sober-minded; be watchful. Your adversary the devil prowls around like a roaring lion, seeking someone to devour" (1 Pet. 5:8 ESV). Our enemy attacks our thoughts, which is why we are told to take our thoughts captive. "We destroy arguments and every lofty opinion raised against the knowledge of God, and take every thought captive to obey Christ" (2 Cor. 10:5 ESV).

As we endeavor to trust God more quickly and completely, we can be confident that he will be true to his Word, he is completely in control, he already knows the outcome, he is sovereign, and he has shown himself repeatedly good and true in others' lives and in our own. In trusting God completely and receiving his power, love, and sound mind, we shed worry, anxiety, and fear, and peace prevails!

Your Rx

1. Look up the following verses: Joshua 1:9; Psalm 56:3; 112:8; and Romans 8:6. Then write them on index cards and place them where you will see them frequently. Read each of these passages aloud three times daily, committing them to memory.

2. Take some time to record in a journal or your Bible the times God has proven his trustworthiness in your life. Thank him for those times.

3. Review the nine ways to operate with a sound mind. Prayerfully commit to one new way you will begin operating with a sound mind in order to overcome worry, anxiety, and fear.

My Prayer for You

Father, we thank you for giving us a sound mind, the mind of Christ. We offer to you all our worries, anxieties, and fears in exchange for your peace, which prevails through your power, love, and sound mind. Help us to rest in your presence. Help us to remain alert to the enemy's lies, trust your Word, believe your promises, and receive your peace. Thank you that you are 100 percent for us and that outcomes don't depend on us but on your sovereign will, way, and timing. In Jesus's name, amen.

Recommended Playlist

"You Satisfy My Soul," Laura Hackett, © 2012 by Forerunner Music

"Hostage of Peace," Tenth Avenue North, ℗ 2012 by Provident Label Group LLC

Living in Peace

Within weeks of turning in the manuscript for the book you hold in your hands to my editor, I was driving with my husband to meet with his oncologist when my doctor called and said the words no one ever wants or expects to hear: "I'm sorry to tell you this, but you have cancer."

I sat stunned for what felt like minutes but could only have been a second or two before responding, "Excuse me? What did you say?"

She repeated, "I'm sorry, but you have cancer. We will need to schedule surgery."

This couldn't be. We were on our way to my husband's oncologist to learn of his health status after his three-time war on cancer.

Thoughts raced through my head. *I wouldn't have been surprised if we had received a bad report from his doctor, but me? I'm healthy. I just went in because the discomfort and bleeding were a nuisance. This can't be. I have things to do. Holidays to prepare for. How can they be sure?*

My thoughts were abruptly brought to a halt when she interrupted, "Could we schedule that now?"

Honestly, I was in such a state of shock that I couldn't think, much less navigate a phone and a calendar at the same time. "Um, I'll have to call you back."

After I hung up, my husband looked at me. "Everything okay?"

In a voice that sounded foreign to my own ears, I relayed what I had just been told. He had questions I couldn't answer. I had even more questions. We would have to just sit with them and make it through his appointment.

We sat waiting to see his doctor, holding hands and drawing strength from each other. At one point, I realized I had been holding my breath and had to intentionally remind myself to breathe. We sat in silence, neither one of us saying a word and yet knowing the other's thoughts. The conversation with the doctor replayed over and over in my mind. *Where do we go from here?* I wondered.

It was then that I realized I had a choice. I could slip down that slippery slope into worry, anxiety, and fear, or I could claim God's peace. I had just turned in the manuscript for this book about exchanging our worries, fears, and anxieties for God's peace, and I guess the enemy wanted to know if I believed my message.

I remembered these truths:

- Even though I was stunned, this did not take God by surprise (Jer. 29:11).
- God is still on his throne, and he is still in the miracle-making business (Ps. 47:8).
- "I will not die but live, and will proclaim what the LORD has done" (Ps. 118:17).
- Jesus warned that we would have trials in this life, but he has overcome them all (John 16:33).
- "When I am weak, then I am strong" (2 Cor. 12:10).
- No weapon formed against me shall prevail (Isa. 54:17).
- By his stripes I am healed (Isa. 53:5).
- God has always been faithful before, and I have no reason to doubt him now (Deut. 7:9).
- "The LORD is close to the brokenhearted and saves those who are crushed in spirit" (Ps. 34:18).

- God's plans are to prosper me and not to harm me, and they include a future and a hope (Jer. 29:11).
- God promised that he who began a good work in me will see it through to completion (Phil. 1:6).
- I do not need to be afraid, because God will be with me wherever I go (Josh. 1:9).
- Greater is he who is in me than he who is in the world (1 John 4:4).
- God will fight this battle for me, if I will only be still (Exod. 14:14).
- God will use even this for good and for his glory (Rom. 8:28).
- God has not given me the spirit of fear but instead power, love, and a sound mind (2 Tim. 1:7).
- God will be my comforter through this so that I can then comfort others with the comfort he has given me (2 Cor. 1:3–4).
- Ultimately, my hope comes from God. Because of him, hope prevails (Ps. 62:5).

As I thought about these truths, I remembered the importance of knowing what we believe before a crisis hits so that when it does, our core beliefs will sustain us during the difficult times. Within a minute, I had to decide whether I was going to believe all the lies swirling around in my head and cave in to worry, anxiety, and fear, or whether I was going to find comfort in my long-standing beliefs in a good, loving, trustworthy God and maintain my peace.

I chose to stand on these truths and rest in the knowledge that God is in control and that I am safe in the shelter of his wing.

This is exactly what we've discussed throughout this book. When the spirit of fear comes to taunt and haunt us, we can choose to refute his lies with God's truth. Then we can maintain our peace because we trust God to be true to his Word.

195

I pray you don't need to experience something as difficult as a cancer diagnosis to help you decide whether to give in to worry, anxiety, and fear or maintain your peace. But when you trust in the goodness and faithfulness of a trustworthy God and know that the enemy is a liar, you can choose to whom you'd rather surrender. You can refuse to give in to worry, anxiety, and fear because God loves you so much and promises to care for you, provide for you, protect you, comfort you, and be your refuge. Knowing he has your back and wants the best for you will allow you to rest in his peace.

May it be well with your soul, and may you reside in his peace today and each day forward. Your body, mind, and spirit will thank you.

With him, peace prevails!
Dr. Michelle

I created for you a free printable list of Scripture passages to help you combat worry, anxiety, and fear: https://drmichellebengtson.com /scriptures-combat-worry-fear-anxiety/.

Acknowledgments

Scott—Words cannot adequately express how grateful I am that you are my husband. How do you thank someone for believing in you when you didn't believe in yourself, reminding you of truth in love, and encouraging you so your dreams gain wings? Without your love and support, none of my dreams of writing books or speaking would have come to fruition. Everyone should be so blessed.

Blake and Bryce—In the game of "I love you more," I love you most! Of all the hats I wear (doctor, author, speaker . . .) I'm most blessed to be called Mom by two amazing, hardworking, God-fearing men. He has already begun a good work in you both, and I cannot wait to watch as he perfects it and uses you for the kingdom in your adult lives.

Janis—I could never have foreseen how much I'd enjoy working with you and just how much I needed your assistance. You always represent me well, with the positivity and encouragement this encourager's heart needs.

Charley and Karen—Thank you for your unconditional love and support and for offering me a place to retreat while under the covering of your prayers. Karen, I will forever fondly remember researching side by side and breaking for the much-coveted couch time.

Gene and Sheila—Words cannot convey what it means to me to have been welcomed into your family. Thank you for opening your home for me to sequester and immerse myself in writing without distraction while enjoying the occasional meal or ice cream run and being close enough to see my #PilotMan.

Peg and Gina—Everyone should have their own personal Aaron and Hur as loving, protective, and uplifting as you two. You bring joy and laughter to my life.

Diana—You offered to spearhead a prayer team before I ever realized how vital that would be. Thank you hardly seems enough. It's been the prayers of others that have lent me strength on the hardest of days.

MaryLee—I will never know how to adequately thank you for your ready willingness to help with research, lend an editorial eye on short notice, encourage the #HopePrevails Community, and pray me through the submission finishing line.

Mother Maxi—Thoughts of your highlighting and red check marks often helped me focus on my readers throughout the writing of this book. Your Sunday hugs and your frequent prayers encouraged my heart beyond words.

Tawny—I love how God orders our steps, and I thank him for a "chance" encounter over lunch that has produced fruit for the kingdom.

Vicki—Every writer should be so blessed to have a keen but encouraging editor like you. Your interest in this project and your willingness to see me through the difficult days were great motivators. Looking forward to our next chance to catch up in person and hopefully many more books to come.

My Hope Ambassadors—I could not get the word out without you. You are helping to fulfill God's promise to spread his Word to the nations. You are such a faithful and encouraging group. I wish you all lived close enough for me to give you a grateful hug.

The #HopePrevails Community on Facebook—I love each of you. It thrills my heart as you share of your lives within the community, offer prayerful support for one another, and together help us remember God's faithfulness. That's how hope is meant to be shared.

All those who submitted their stories for consideration—I am both humbled and grateful for your willingness to share in order to help others. I only wish I could have fit in every story. So often what we see as messes in our own lives are the perfect ministry to others' lives. May you be blessed beyond measure.

My readers—This book would not have been written if it weren't for you. This is the book, and the very topic, you asked for. I continually kept you in mind as I sought the Lord for a word for you to positively impact your lives and your hearts. May you enter into a season fully walking in power, love, a sound mind, and peace provided to you by the Lover of your souls.

Notes

Chapter 1 The Elephant in the Room

1. *Diagnostic and Statistical Manual of Mental Disorders*, 5th ed. (Arlington, VA: American Psychiatric Association, 2013), 189.

2. *Merriam-Webster*, s.v. "worry," accessed January 24, 2019, https://www.merriam -webster.com/dictionary/worry.

3. *Merriam-Webster*, s.v. "anxiety," accessed January 24, 2019, https://www.merriam -webster.com/dictionary/anxiety.

4. Vanessa Coppard-Queensland, "Globally 1 in 13 Suffers from Anxiety," Futurity, September 5, 2012, https://www.futurity.org/globally-1-in-13-suffers-from-anxiety/.

5. R. C. Kessler et al., "The Global Burden of Mental Disorders: An Update from the WHO World Mental Health (WMH) Surveys," *Epidemiologia e psichiatria sociale* 18, no. 1 (2009): 23–33.

6. A. J. Baxter et al., "Global Prevalence of Anxiety Disorders: A Systematic Review and Meta-regression," *Psychological Medicine* 43, no. 5 (May 2013), https://www .cambridge.org/core/journals/psychological-medicine/article/global-prevalence -of-anxiety-disorders-a-systematic-review-and-metaregression/484845CE01E709 EE4FB6554AA78E612F.

7. Coppard-Queensland, "Globally 1 in 13 Suffers from Anxiety."

8. "Health Statistics and Information Systems," World Health Organization, accessed March 20, 2019, https://www.who.int/healthinfo/global_burden_dis ease/estimates/en/.

9. "Depression and Other Common Mental Disorders: Global Health Estimates," World Health Organization, 2017, https://apps.who.int/iris/bitstream/10665/25 4610/1/WHO-MSD-MER-2017.2-eng.pdf?ua=1.

10. "Any Anxiety Disorder," National Institute of Mental Health, updated November 2017, https://www.nimh.nih.gov/health/statistics/prevalence/any-anxiety -disorder-among-adults.shtml.

11. C. Lindsay DeVane, PharmD, et al., "Anxiety Disorders in the 21st Century: Status, Challenges, Opportunities, and Comorbidity With Depression," AJMC 11, no. 12 (October 20, 2005): s344–53, https://www.ajmc.com/journals/supplement /2005/2005-10-vol11-n12suppl/oct05-2158ps344-s353.

12. "Facts and Statistics," Anxiety and Depression Association of America, accessed March 20, 2019, https://www.adaa.org/about-adaa/press-room/facts-statistics.

13. https://adaa.org/about-adaa/press-room/facts-statistics.

14. Carmen P. McLean et al., "Gender Differences in Anxiety Disorders: Prevalence, Course of Illness, Comorbidity and Burden of Illness," *Journal of Psychiatric Research* 45, no. 8 (August 2011): 1027–35, doi:10.1016/j.jpsychires.2011.03.006.

15. "Why Do So Many Women Have Anxiety Disorders? A Hormone Hypothesis," CommonHealth, April 23, 2005, https://www.wbur.org/commonhealth/2015 /04/23/women-anxiety-hormones.

16. Borwin Bandelow, MD, PhD, and Sophie Michaelis, MD, "Epidemiology of Anxiety Disorders in the 21st Century," *Dialogues in Clinical Neuroscience* 17, no. 3 (September 2015): 327–35, https://www.ncbi.nlm.nih.gov/pmc/articles/PMC 4610617/.

17. "Health Statistics and Information Systems."

18. *Merriam-Webster*, s.v. "fear," accessed January 24, 2019, https://www.merriam -webster.com/dictionary/fear.

19. "Over 200 Recognized Phobias," PsychCentral, accessed January 24, 2019, https://forums.psychcentral.com/anxiety-panic-phobias/25437-over-200-recog nized-phobias.html.

20. "Worry, Anxiety, Fear, or Panic," Psychology Solution, accessed January 24, 2019, https://www.psychology-solution.com/anxiety/worry-anxiety-fear-panic.

21. *Merriam-Webster*, s.v. "peace," accessed January 24, 2019, https://www.merriam -webster.com/dictionary/peace.

22. https://philosiblog.com/2013/06/19/if-you-are-depressed-you-are-living -in-the-past-if-you-are-anxious-living-in-the-future-if-you-are-at-peace-you-are -living-in-the-moment/.

23. David Jeremiah Quotes, accessed January 24, 2019, https://www.bestquotes 4ever.com/authors/david-jeremiah-quotes.

Chapter 2 Why Me?

1. Dictionary.com, s.v. "rest," accessed January 24, 2019, https://www.dictionary.com /browse/rest.

Chapter 3 Fear Lurks

1. Karl Albrecht, "The (Only) Five Basic Fears We All Live By," Goodreads, March 14, 2014, https://www.goodreads.com/author_blog_posts/5913256-the -only-five-basic-fears-we-all-live-by.

2. "Ralph Waldo Emerson Quotes," Goodreads, accessed January 24, 2019, https://www.goodreads.com/quotes/309832-fear-defeats-more-people-than-any -other-one-thing-in.

3. Michelle Bengtson, *Hope Prevails: Insights from a Doctor's Personal Journey through Depression* (Grand Rapids: Revell, 2016).

4. "Naguib Mahfouz Quotes," Goodreads, accessed January 24, 2019, https://www.goodreads.com/quotes/6822313-fear-doesn-t-prevent-death-it-prevents-life.

5. Julia Keller, "The Mysterious Ambrose Redmoon's Healing Words," *Chicago Tribune*, March 29, 2002, https://articles.chicagotribune.com/2002-03-29/features/0203290018_1_chicago-police-officer-terry-hillard-courage.

Chapter 4 Worry Creeps

1. QuoteFancy, accessed January 24, 2019, https://quotefancy.com/quote/1510677/Esther-Hicks-Worrying-is-using-your-imagination-to-create-something-you-don-t-want.

Chapter 6 Crises Explode

1. Michelle Bengtson, *Hope Prevails Bible Study: Insights from a Doctor's Personal Journey through Depression* (Enumclaw, Washington: Redemption Press, 2017).

2. https://www.barrons.com/articles/hank-paulson-looks-backat-the-turmoil-of-2008-1536759000

3. BibleHub, s.v. "samak," accessed January 24, 2019, https://biblehub.com/hebrew/5564.htm.

4. BibleHub, s.v. "yetser," accessed January 24, 2019, https://biblehub.com/hebrew/3336.htm.

5. BibleHub, s.v. "natsar," accessed January 24, 2019, https://biblehub.com/hebrew/5341.htm.

6. "Bald Eagle Facts: Q&A with Peter Nye in 2007 New York Department of Environmental Conservation," Journey North, https://journeynorth.org/tm/eagle/ExpertAnswer07.html.

Chapter 8 God Is

1. "When Peace, Like a River," Hymnary.org, accessed January 24, 2019, https://hymnary.org/text/when_peace_like_a_river_attendeth_my_way.

2. PassItOn.com, accessed January 24, 2019, https://www.passiton.com/inspirational-quotes/7228-peace-it-does-not-mean-to-be-in-a-place-where.

3. Pinterest, accessed January 24, 2019, https://www.pinterest.com/pin/64246732160024962/.

Chapter 10 Live in His Perfect Love

1. "Crazy Love with Francis Chan," Bible.com, accessed January 24, 2019, https://www.bible.com/reading-plans/1285-crazy-love-with-francis-chan/day/2#!.

Chapter 11 Use Your Sound Mind

1. Indulgy, accessed January 24, 2019, https://indulgy.com/post/qELNw95D04/your-faith-can-move-mountains-and-your-doubt-ca.

Dr. Michelle Bengtson is a board-certified neuropsychologist with more than twenty-five years of experience in mental health. She is an international speaker as well as a national and international media resource on mental health, spiritual well-being, and wellness. Dr. Bengtson is the author of the award-winning *Hope Prevails: Insights From a Doctor's Personal Journey through Depression* and *Hope Prevails Bible Study*. She writes at www.drmichellebengtson.com, for Roma Downey and Mark Burnett's LightWorkers.com, Liberty in Christ Ministries, and For God's Glory Alone Ministries. She is also host of the weekly radio/podcast program *Your Hope Filled Perspective with Dr. Michelle Bengtson*, which can be found at www.graceandtruth radio.world/shows/your-hope-filled-perspective. She lives in Dallas/Fort Worth with her husband of more than thirty years, their two sons, and three dogs.

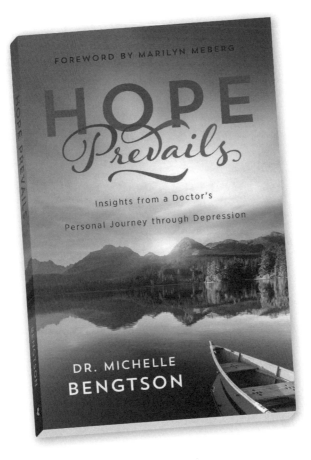